Living with Bipolar Disorder

Living with Bipolar Disorder

A Guide for Individuals and Families

Michael W. Otto
Noreen A. Reilly-Harrington
Robert O. Knauz
Aude Henin
Jane N. Kogan
Gary S. Sachs

OXFORD
UNIVERSITY PRESS

2008

OXFORD
UNIVERSITY PRESS

Oxford University Press, Inc., publishes works that further
Oxford University's objective of excellence
in research, scholarship, and education.

Oxford   New York

Auckland   Cape Town   Dar es Salaam   Hong Kong   Karachi
Kuala Lumpur   Madrid   Melbourne   Mexico City   Nairobi
New Delhi   Shanghai   Taipei   Toronto

With offices in

Argentina   Austria   Brazil   Chile   Czech Republic   France   Greece
Guatemala   Hungary   Italy   Japan   Poland   Portugal   Singapore
South Korea   Switzerland   Thailand   Turkey   Ukraine   Vietnam

Copyright © 2008 by Oxford University Press, Inc.

Published by Oxford University Press, Inc.
198 Madison Avenue, New York, New York 10016
www.oup.com

Oxford is a registered trademark of Oxford University Press

ISBN-13: 9780195323580 Paper

1 3 5 7 9 8 6 4 2

Printed in the United States of America

on acid-free paper

Dedications

MWO: For my son, Jackson, a source of unending joy

NR-H: With all my love for my husband, Joe, and our three beautiful sons, Joseph, Kevin, & Owen

ROK: To my son, Alex who reminds me to dream big every day.

AH: For my husband Sean and son Maxim, with all my love

JNK: To the brightest lights in my life, Henry and Nora, with love

GSS: To Maryanne, your grace, support, and humor are the enduring treasures of my life.

Contents

Acknowledgments

This book was designed for individuals with bipolar disorder, their families, and clinicians who help their patients manage the disorder. It provides useful information and strategies that everyone affected by this disorder should have. The interventions included in this book were shaped by our collaborations with a number of teams of clinicians and clinical researchers as well as by the patients with whom we have worked. In particular, we would like to thank and acknowledge the input of our colleagues in the very large, NIMH-funded, Systematic Treatment Enhancement Program for Bipolar Disorder (STEP-BD). Our perspectives on treatment were further influenced by independent studies led by Ellen Frank, Dominic Lam, David Miklowitz, and Jan Scott. Likewise, we learned the value of attending to the promotion of wellbeing from research by Giovanni Fava. Useful comments on early versions of this book were provided by a variety of members of the STEP-BD program, including valued feedback from David Miklowitz and Ellen Frank. We thank all of these individuals for expanding what is known about the nature and treatment of bipolar disorder.

Living with Bipolar Disorder

Part 1

Understanding Bipolar Disorder and Its Treatment

1

Introduction

This book provides you with a wealth of information on the nature and treatment of bipolar disorder as well as strategies designed to reduce the likelihood of future episodes of depression or mania. In addition to written information, separate Self-Guided Care boxes are used to provide you with opportunities to rehearse self-care activities. These are designed to help you be an active force in coping with your disorder and enhancing your enjoyment of life. Also, all of the strategies in this book are designed for use in conjunction with your treatment team—the doctors, therapists, family members, and others you select as your support system. Near the end of this book, you will be asked to create a treatment contract to inform your treatment team and your support network how to recognize possible periods of illness and the strategies you want them to use to take good care of you.

To get the most benefit from this book, take your time reading and, if you wish, jump from chapter to chapter to focus on those sections most relevant to you at any given time. We would, however, like you to devote time to every chapter of the book to get the most of the strategies and information provided to enhance your control of bipolar disorder. In addition, use the information provided to be a better consumer of the treatments available to you and a better contributor to the treatment decision-making process.

One of the first suggestions for you as an active collaborator in your treatment is to begin thinking about building your support network. Namely, with whom do you want to share this book? The goal is to make your support team even more valuable to you by giving them information about bipolar disorder and a common vocabulary for discussing treatment. Having the family members and friends that you choose read the book is one way to make them more valuable collaborators in your care. Take some time to think about whom you would like to be a part of your support network, and begin to fill out the first Self-Guided Care box.

Self-Guided Care: Selecting Members of Your Support Group

Who might you select because they are supportive individuals?

_____

_____

_____

Who might you select because they have an important impact on your life?

_____

_____

_____

Who might you select in order to improve their understanding of bipolar disorder and how to be helpful to you?

_____

_____

_____

2
Description of Bipolar Disorder

Bipolar disorder, also known as manic depression, is a common psychiatric disorder. It is one of several conditions referred to as *mood disorders,* which are diagnosed based on the occurrence of episodes. Understanding the concept of an episode is important for understanding mood disorders. A mood episode refers to a set of symptoms that occur during the same time period. This simple definition is made more complex because the set of symptoms used to make the diagnosis can include many different combinations of symptoms. For example, mood episodes can be understood much like an episode in a weekly television show. We can think of symptoms like the cast of characters. In this example, mood symptoms are the leading players, but to be recognizable as an episode of a specific show, the presence of other supporting actors is required. Although the entire cast may never be present in the same scene, and some actors may appear in more than one show, we can usually recognize a specific show by the appearance of any combination of a small number of cast members. Once we recognize the show, however, an episode can be said to continue

> *Bipolar disorder is also known as manic depression and is a common psychiatric disorder.*

for as long as the lead player and/or the supporting cast maintain a significant presence on the stage.

Most clinicians diagnose psychiatric problems by using a manual referred to as *DSM–IV–TR* (*Diagnostic and Statistical Manual*, 4th edition, text revision), which defines the symptom characteristics of each disorder. The *DSM–IV–TR* provides specific sets of symptoms that define episodes of depression, hypomania, mania, and mixed episodes. Throughout the rest of this chapter you will find an overview of the *DSM–IV–TR* concepts most likely to be used by your doctor.

What Is Mania?

Mania is more than just having a lot of energy or feeling great about yourself. Mania is a serious condition that is diagnosed when a person experiences several symptoms associated with an elevated or high mood that go beyond what most people experience. Mania includes symptoms such as increased energy, racing thoughts, inflated self-esteem, a decreased need for sleep, abnormal irritability, extreme happiness, poor judgment, and overparticipation in risky activities. These symptoms must be present during a period of least one week to be considered mania (see Table 2.1 for more details).

For many people, the initial symptoms of mania may feel pleasurable, however, an episode of abnormal mood elevation often causes serious disruption to an individual's normal life plans and goals. When mania causes an individual's thinking to be overly positive and impairs judgment, actions are not evaluated thoroughly and negative financial, career, or relationship consequences may follow. Mania often is associated with significant and sometimes severe problems in daily living. Sometimes the problems are so severe that a person must be hospitalized. Even when mania does not result in hospitalization, it may cause great upheavals in a person's life.

Table 2.1 Summary of DSM-IV-TR Episodes

Episode type	Predominant mood state	Duration	Associated features
Mania	High, happy, euphoric, expansive, irritable	At least one week	1. Increased self esteem/grandiosity 2. Decreased need for sleep 3. More talkative 4. Racing thought/flight of ideas 5. Distractible 6. Increased goal-directed activities/psychomotor agitation 7. Risk-taking
Hypomania	High, happy, euphoric, expansive, irritable	At least four days	1. Increased self-esteem/grandiosity 2. Decreased need for sleep 3. More talkative 4. Racing thoughts/flight of ideas 5. Distractible 6. Increased goal-directed activities/psychomotor agitation 7. Risk-taking
Depression	Low, sad, disinterested	At least two weeks	1. Sleep disturbance 2. Diminished interest 3. Guilt/low self-esteem 4. Decreased energy 5. Inability to concentrate/make simple decisions 6. Appetite disturbance 7. Psychomotor retardation/agitation 8. Suicidal ideation/morbid preoccupation
Mixed	High, happy, euphoric, expansive, irritable, low, sad, disinterested	At least one week	Associated features present that fulfill both mania and depression.

What Is Hypomania?

The term *hypomania* refers to a clearly abnormal mood state with mild to severe symptoms of mania that may last for a few days or may persist for many months. The key differences between mania and hypomania are both the severity of symptoms and, more importantly, the effect the symptoms have on your life (see Table 2.1 for more details). Mania can cause enormous problems in daily functioning and often leads to serious problems with a person's relationships or work functioning.

By definition, hypomania does not cause problems to the same extent as mania, and for some patients hypomania can be a pleasant state of good humor and high productivity. Unfortunately, for most people hypomania can be problematic. Things said and done during a hypomanic episode often have negative long-term consequences. For example, during a hypomanic episode, buying more clothes than necessary might delay rent or mortgage payments, or telling off-color jokes might bring attention at the office party but lessen the chances for promotion in the long run. Hypomania often occurs just before or immediately after other severe mood states. A hypomanic phase can be coupled with full manic episodes or it can occur at the beginning or end of a severe depression. In other words, a hypomanic episode may be a sign that a more severe manic episode is on the way, or it may be a sign that a person is going to "crash" and become depressed.

What Is Depression?

An episode of major depression, often simply referred to as *depression* is more than just the sad mood most people might experience when they have had a bad day. Major depression is a medical disorder that lasts at least two weeks and produces a combination of physical and emotional symptoms that make it very difficult to function in life (see Table 2.1 for more details).

At the heart of clinical depression is a loss of pleasure in activities that used to be fun or exciting. Also, people often have feelings of sadness, hopelessness, and pessimism. These symptoms are accompanied by a wide variety of physical symptoms such as difficulty sleeping, poor concentration and memory, low energy, and change in appetite. Not everyone will experience all of these physical symptoms. For example, someone may have problems with their sleep and feel low in energy but their appetite may remain normal. Depression also changes the way a person thinks about the world. For example, it is not uncommon for people who are depressed to feel helpless and hopeless about their life situation, and, at times, people may feel that suicide is a rational alternative to their current situation (see Chapter 8). With time, it may be difficult to remember that depression is treatable.

Unipolar and Bipolar Mood Disorders

The *DSM–IV–TR* classifies mood disorders into two main types, unipolar and bipolar, which are based largely on which types of episodes have been diagnosed. Although unipolar and bipolar disorders are both considered mood disorders, they are different illnesses. Patients are diagnosed with unipolar disorders if they have only experienced episodes of depressed mood. They never experience the manic or hypomanic symptoms of bipolar disorder.

Subtypes of Bipolar Disorder

There are four subtypes of bipolar disorder: Bipolar I, Bipolar II, Cyclothymia, and Bipolar NOS (not otherwise specified).

> *Bipolar I* refers to a condition in which patients have experienced one or more episodes of mania (see Table 2.2 for more details). Although you do not need an episode of depression to get a diagnosis of Bipolar I, most people who have Bipolar I experience episodes of both mania and depression. In other words,

Table 2.2 *Summary of Unipolar and Bipolar Disorders*

	Mania	Hypomania	Depression
Unipolar disorders			
Major depression	No	No	Yes
Dysthymic disorder	No	No	No, but person feels chronically sad or down
Bipolar disorders			
Bipolar I	Yes	Yes	Usually
Bipolar II	No	Yes	Yes
Cyclothymia	No	Yes	No, but person has periods where they feel sad or down
Bipolar NOS or	No	Yes	Person has some symptoms of depression
Bipolar NOS	No	Person has some symptoms of hypomania	Yes

most patients who have Bipolar I will have episodes of both depression and mania, while a few patients will have episodes of mania alone.

Bipolar II refers to a condition in which patients have had at least one hypomanic episode (see Table 2.2 for more details) but have never experienced a full manic episode. To meet criteria for Bipolar II, a patient also must have had at least one episode of depression.

More than 10 million men and women in the United States have bipolar disorder.

The major difference between Bipolar I and Bipolar II disorders is that Bipolar I requires at least one manic episode, whereas Bipolar II requires that periods of mood elevation meet criteria for hypomania but not necessarily the full criteria for mania. Table 2.2 may help you further understand these distinctions.

Cyclothymia, refers to forms of bipolar illness that include a period of chronic mood instability (one year for children or adolescents, two years for adults). For the majority of the days during this period, patients experience abnormal mood states that must include frequent hypomanic symptoms that never meet full criteria for mania or major depression.

Bipolar NOS (not otherwise specified) refers to periods of clearly abnormal mood elevation that fail to meet criteria for any of the other subtypes. For example, a person can have some symptoms of mood elevation followed by an episode of depression. Because the symptoms of hypomania were too brief or too few to meet the full criteria for hypomania, the person would not qualify for Bipolar II but would qualify for a diagnosis of Bipolar NOS. Also a person with 4 or even 10 hypomanias but no depressions would be diagnosed as Bipolar NOS. Bipolar NOS is sometimes referred to as *Atypical Bipolar* disorder.

In summary, what distinguishes bipolar disorders from unipolar disorders is the occurrence of episodes of abnormally high, expansive, or irritable mood (e.g., hypomania or mania). Episodes of depression (low mood) are also a common feature of bipolar disorder. A person with bipolar disorder may experience mood swings from excessive highs (mania) to profound hopelessness (depression), usually with periods of normal mood in between. Some individuals experience mixed episodes in which symptoms of both mania and depression occur at the same time.

How Common Is Bipolar Disorder?

Approximately 1%–5% of adults in the population have bipolar disorder. In the United States alone, more than 10 million people have bipolar disorder. Overall, the disorder affects both women and men equally. Bipolar disorder also affects adolescents and children; information on managing the disorder in this age range is provided in Chapter 6.

What Is the Course of the Disorder?

Bipolar disorder can occur at any time but usually begins before age 35. People between the ages of 15–25 have the highest risk of developing this disorder. However, the delay between the first signs and symptoms of the disorder and proper diagnosis and treatment is often 10 years.

The type, severity, and duration of mood episodes can vary. For example, some individuals may have more manic episodes or more depressed episodes, whereas others may have an equal number of depressive and manic episodes. The length of time that someone is in a normal mood state after an episode also can vary greatly. Without treatment, the patient experiences shorter periods of normal mood and experiences more periods of depression, hypomania, and mania. For most patients this increase in mood episodes ends after three to five episodes. During a 10-year period, the average bipolar patient will have about four mood episodes.

Approximately one out of eight individuals with bipolar disorder suffer from the *rapid cycling* form of the disorder (i.e., four or more mood episodes per year). Rapid cycling tends to be more common in women than in men. If a woman experiences an episode of bipolar disorder within four weeks after childbirth, that episode can be designated as having a postpartum onset. Some people also experience a seasonal pattern to bipolar disorder, where most episodes start and end around the same time each year.

Even among patients who have frequent severe episodes there may be long periods of a normal mood state. Some doctors, patients, and family members may be tempted to interpret these periods of wellness as evidence that the diagnosis of bipolar disorder was incorrect. Unfortunately, this is seldom the case. Bipolar disorder often has natural periods of remission, but those who meet criteria for bipolar disorder will almost always relapse without treatment.

What Causes Bipolar Disorder?

Bipolar disorder is likely caused by multiple factors that interact with each other. It often runs in families and there is a genetic component to the disorder. For example, your chances of getting bipolar disorder are higher if your parents or siblings have this disorder. However, even though someone may have inherited the genes for bipolar disorder, there is no guarantee that this person will develop the disorder. A stressful environment or negative life events may interact with an underlying genetic or biological vulnerability to produce the disorder. In other words, some people are born with genes that make it more likely that they will get bipolar disorder. It is not known why some people with these genes develop bipolar disorder and others do not. Often, a stressful event seems to trigger the first episode. Therefore, an individual's coping skills or style for handling stress also may play a role in the development of symptoms. In some cases, drug abuse (e.g., alcohol, amphetamines, LSD, cocaine, etc.) can trigger the disorder. Stressful life events also may lead to a loss of sleep or a change in usual routines. Such changes in one's schedule can contribute to the onset and recurrence of depression and mania.

Comorbidity

Comorbidity is a psychiatric term that refers to a situation in which a person has two or more psychiatric disorders that often occur at the same time. The *DSM–IV* lists more than 330 different types of psychiatric disorders. A person with bipolar disorder is very likely to meet the criteria for one or more additional disorders. No one knows why, but having bipolar disorder appears to make you more vulnerable to anxiety disorders, alcoholism, substance abuse, bulimia, attention deficit disorder, and migraine headaches. Successful treatment of bipolar disorder almost always improves these other conditions. Likewise, successful treatment of these conditions usually improves the symptoms of bipolar disorder. Unfortunately for some patients, the treatments for other disorders can worsen symptoms of bipolar disorder. For example, the medicines used to treat obsessive-compulsive disorder (antidepressants) and attention deficit disorder (stimulants) may worsen symptoms of bipolar disorder and even cause a manic episode. When this happens it is usually possible to find other treatments that help these conditions.

Factors in Coping with Bipolar Disorder

Some of the strategies that protect you from future episodes include: taking medications appropriately; using social, family, and community

Table 2.3 *Protective and Risk Factors in Bipolar Disorder*

Protective factors	Risk factors
■ Use of mood stabilizing medications	■ Alcohol
■ Abstinence from alcohol	■ Recreational drugs
■ Abstinence from recreational drug use	■ Abrupt discontinuation of medications
■ Structured schedule	■ Mood stabilizers
■ Regular awake and sleep times	■ Antidepressants
■ Schedule of recurring social activity	■ Anxiolytics
■ Support system	■ Sleep disruption
■ Professionals	■ Loss of supports
■ Family	■ Cognitive distortions
■ Friends	■ Interpersonal conflict
■ Psychotherapy	■ Role transition
	■ Negative emotional communications
	■ East–west travel
	■ Anxiety disorders and stress

supports; using communication or problem-solving skills; and utilizing treatment resources such as psychotherapy. Throughout this book we will present strategies that utilize these protective factors while avoiding risk factors (see Table 2.3 for a list of protective versus risk factors).

Medication Names and Common Dosages

This chapter reviews the medications commonly used to treat bipolar disorder. As an active participant in your treatment, it is important for you to know the purpose as well as the proper dosage, side effects, and schedule for each medication you use. This information makes it easier for you and your doctor to select and adjust medications in a manner that most benefits you. Please discuss your concerns about medication with your physician. Your doctor will be able to help you cope with the side effects or consider alternative treatments.

> *If you have bipolar disorder, it is important that you know the proper dosage and potential side effects of your medication.*

Do I Really Need to Take Medications?

Many individuals have mixed feelings about taking medications, and, in an ideal world, most people would choose not to do so. However, numerous studies have shown the benefit of medications for treating episodes of depression and mania and helping to prevent these episodes. Medications, such as mood stabilizers and antidepressants, can be thought of as tools that help you feel better and help you take control of your life.

What Types of Medications are Used to Treat Bipolar Disorder?

The following sections describe the four major types of medications used to treat bipolar disorder: mood stabilizers, antidepressants, antipsychotics, and antianxiety (anxiolytics). These medications are the main tools for controlling bipolar disorder. Used individually or in combination, these medications provide a way for you to manage your bipolar disorder. Other medication tools also may be used to treat additional symptoms.

Before we describe in more detail the types of medication, their purposes, and some side effects, we should first provide some important information about the *names* of these classes of medication.

Drugs often are classified according to the purpose for which they *first* got approval for use in the United States. Although many drugs are found to have a variety of uses in addition to this first use, the original name sticks. Because of this, doctors often use drugs classified as *antidepressants* to treat anxiety and drugs called *anxiolytics* to treat insomnia. For this reason, it is extremely important for you to know the purpose of a medication, not just its name. It helps to try to have a sense of humor with the well-meaning people who may question your medications because they take these classification terms at face value. For example, a family member may wonder why you are taking a medication for anxiety when you have bipolar disorder. Similar questions about your medication may arise when you pick up your medications at the pharmacy, when you share the names of the medications with your friends or family, or even when you see your primary care physician. When there are questions about your medication, speak to your doctor before you make any changes.

Mood Stabilizers

The goal of treatment with mood stabilizers is to keep your mood within a normal range. While experts agree that mood stabilizers are the best treatment for bipolar disorder, the term *mood stabilizer* is not a precisely defined scientific term. There is general agreement among experts that lithium (e.g., Eskalith and Lithobid), valproate (Depakote), lamotrigine (e.g., Lamictal), carbamazepine (Tegretol), and olanazpine (Zyprexa) are mood stabilizers. Each of these drugs has been shown to be an effective treatment for mania and/or relapse prevention in two or more rigorous studies. There are numerous studies showing that lithium is effective for preventing relapse and for the treatment of bipolar depression. Several studies have shown lamotrigine can be an effective for treatment of bipolar depression and two have shown benefit for relapse prevention, particularly for prevention of depressive recurrence. Olanzapine has demonstrated excellent benefits against acute mania, has some antidepressant benefit, and appears to be particularly useful for preventing manic relapse.

Other drugs may also possess mood-stabilizing properties. Calling a drug a mood stabilizer or a possible mood stabilizer is appropriate if the drug: (1) works as a treatment for mania, depression, or as a prevention of relapse; and (2) does not increase a patient's rate of mood cycling or cause a switch from one abnormal mood state to another. Medications sometimes used by experts as mood stabilizers include Calan, Isoptin, Trileptal, and Omega-3 fatty acids, but these options should be regarded as unproven. None of these have yet proven benefit in a rigorous study or been granted FDA approval for treatment of any aspect of bipolar disorder.

All medications can cause side effects. The goal is for you to work with your physician to find a mood stabilizer that best protects you or helps you

> *All medications can cause side effects.*

recover from episodes of depression or mania, without giving you side effects that are too bothersome.

Antidepressants

A wide range of antidepressants may be administered to treat a depressive episode in bipolar disorder. However, their use must be carefully monitored. Some depressed bipolar patients will switch from depression to mania when treated with standard antidepressant medication. In other words, the antidepressant tool, while sometimes useful for controlling depression, may overshoot a normal mood and cause you to become manic. In contrast, some bipolar patients who are on antidepressants do not experience a switch to mania but suffer a worsening of their depression or more depressive episodes. For this reason, both regular communication and follow-up with your physician are necessary to be sure you are not being made worse off by your treatment. Your physician will monitor you for the emergence of manic symptoms, but he or she can do a much better job with assistance from you and other members of your support team.

Talk to your physician about how you are feeling. If you notice feelings of restlessness, difficulty sleeping, excessive talkativeness, racing thoughts, or a sense of agitation during your antidepressant treatment, make sure you report these symptoms to your physician immediately.

Although a low level of mood elevation may be enjoyable, you do not want these symptoms to escalate into mania. Remember that mania is characterized as a disorder because of the problems it causes in your life. To keep control of your life and your ability to seek and follow your goals, report any early symptoms of mania or hypomania to your physician. With monitoring and care, antidepressant medication can be a valuable addition to your toolbox for treating your bipolar depression.

Table 3.1 provides a list of antidepressant medications. You will note that Wellbutrin-SR and Paxil are listed first because these medications have been studied as a treatment specifically for bipolar depression and appear less likely to cause mania than some older antidepressant medications.

Table 3.1 *Common Medications for Bipolar Disorder: Antidepressants*

Generic name	Trade name	*Common starting daily dose*	*Common daily dose range*
Antidepressants			
Bupropion	Wellbutrin-SR	100 mg	300 mg
Paroxetine	Paxil	10–20 mg	20 mg
Sertraline	Zoloft	50 mg	50–200 mg
Fluvoxamine	Luvox	25–50 mg	150–300 mg
Fluoxetine	Prozac	20 mg	20–60mg
Citalopram	Celexa	20 mg	20–40 mg
Escitalopram	Lexapro	10 mg	10–40 mg
Venlafaxine	Effexor	25–37.5 mg	75–150 mg
Nefazodone	Serzone	100 mg	300–600 mg
Mirtazapine	Remeron	15 mg	15–60 mg
Trazodone	Desyrel	50 mg	300–600 mg
Phenelzine	Nardil	15 mg	60–90 mg
Tranylcypromine	Parnate	10 mg	30–40 mg

Antipsychotics

Antipsychotics were first developed as treatment for the hallucinations and delusions caused by schizophrenia. However, antipsychotic medications have been shown to have specific antimanic effects even in manic patients who don't have any symptoms of psychosis. Antipsychotics are frequently prescribed in the context of a manic episode and may be especially helpful in clearing up disorganized or distorted thinking, as well as hallucinations.

A common property of antipsychotic drugs is the ability to block receptors for the chemical, or neurotransmitter, called dopamine.

Too much dopamine in your brain may contribute to some of the symptoms of mania. You may hear some of your physicians use the term *neuroleptics*. These medications are the same as antipsychotics. Older drugs such as Thorazine, Mellaril, Prolixin, Haldol, or Navane are powerful blockers of dopamine. As a class, neuroleptics are considered helpful for acute mania. They often cause side effects, which limits their usefulness. Early in the course of treatment, patients treated with neuroleptics may experience muscle stiffness, tremors, and sometimes restlessness. Long-term use of neuroleptic drugs is associated with potentially irreversible movement disorders such as tardive dyskinesia (TD), a disorder characterized by repetitive, involuntary, purposeless movements.

Newer antipsychotics are now available for your physician to use to treat mania. Clozapine was the first member of a new class of antipsychotics sometimes called atypical antipsychotic medications. This new class of medications also includes risperidone (Risperdal), olanzapine (Zyprexa), quetiapine (Seroquel), ziprasidone (Geodon), and aripiprazole (Abilify). Similar to the older drugs, these newer drugs also block dopamine receptors but with less potency than the older neuroleptic medications. The atypical antipsychotics also block some receptors for another neurotransmitter called serotonin. Drugs with this combination of low potency dopamine blockade and serotonin blockade are much less likely to cause the kind of intolerable side effects seen with older neuroleptics. The atypical antipsychotics are frequently used alone or in combination with mood stabilizers for the treatment of acute mania.

After recovery from a manic episode, it is standard practice to decrease the dosages of antipsychotic medications. However, some patients begin to have manic symptoms soon after the dosages of antipsychotic medication are lowered. These patients may be prescribed antipsychotics on a continual basis to keep mania from coming back. Consequently, antipsychotics can be thought of as a medication for both the immediate treatment of mania and for the prevention of manic or psychotic symptoms.

Anxiolytic (Antianxiety) Medications

Anxiety is a problem that very frequently accompanies episodes of depression or mania. In addition, sleep problems are common in depression, hypomania, and mania. Within the anxiolytic class, the most frequently used medications are benzodiazepines. These medications include Ativan, Klonopin, Valium, and Xanax, and they are used to help treat anxiety and sleeplessness in bipolar disorder. In addition, the benzodiazepines may be used to help control some of the early symptoms of hypomania. All benzodiazepines have the potential to cause physical and psychological dependence or addiction. The potential for abuse seems to be greatest with drugs that produce a quick effect and that are quickly removed from your blood stream, such as alprazolam (Xanax). The potential for abuse seems to be least with benzodiazepines that have a slower effect and spend a longer time in your blood stream, such as clonazepam (Klonopin).

> *All benzodiazepines have the potential to cause physical and psychological dependence or addiction.*

Most standard antidepressant medications appear to have excellent effects on reducing anxiety, but they require several weeks of consistent use to become effective and may cause worsening of bipolar disorder in some patients.

Finding the Correct Dose

Effective treatment depends on finding the correct dose of medication. Finding the right dose for you becomes easier if you take your medications as directed by your doctor and keep him or her informed about your response to the medications. Tables 3.1, 3.2, and 3.3 provide you with some information and dosage ranges on common mood stabilizers, antidepressants, and antipsychotics. Your physician may give you dosages of medication outside of these ranges. These ranges are displayed to give you a frame of reference and to help you take an active role in discussing dosages with your doctor.

Table 3.2 *Common Medications for Bipolar Disorder: Mood Stabilizers*

Generic name	Trade name	Common starting daily dose	Common daily dose range
Mood stabilizers			
Lithium Carbonate	Lithobid/ Eskalith/ Lithonate	600 mg	900–2400 mg
Carbamazepine	Tegretol	400 mg	200–1600 mg
Divalproex	Depakote	750 mg	750–2750 mg
Lamotrigine	Lamictal	12.5*–25 mg	50–400 mg
Olanzapine	Zyprexa	5–15 mg	2.5–20 mg
Possible mood stabilizers			
Oxcarbazepine	Trileptal	150 mg	450–900 mg
Verapamil	Calan	120 mg	120–360 mg
Amlodipine	Norvasc	2.5 mg	2.5–10 mg
Omega-3 fatty acid	(many available)	1,000 mg	3,000–12,000 mg
Inositol	(many available)	5,000 mg	5000–30,000 mg

* Common starting dose for Lamotrigine is 12.5 mg if you also are taking Divalproex, but 25 mg if not prescribed Divalproex.

Table 3.3 *Common Medications for Bipolar Disorder: Antipsychotics*

Generic name	Trade name	Common starting daily dose	Common daily dose range
Antipsychotics			
Clozapine	Clozaril	25 mg	25–400 mg
Risperidone	Risperdal	1.0 mg	0.5–6 mg
Olanzapine	Zyprexa	5–10 mg	2.5–20 mg
Quetiapine	Seroquel	100 mg	25–800 mg
Ziprasidone	Geodon	80 mg	80–240 mg
Aripiprazole	Abilify	5–15 mg	5–30 mg
Trifluoperazine	Stelazine	2–5 mg	5–10 mg
Perphenazine	Trilafon	4 mg	4–32 mg
Haloperidol	Haldol	2 mg	0.5–10 mg

4

Getting in the Habit of Taking Medications

Finding a Reliable Way to Take Your Medications

It is important that you develop a habit of taking your pills regularly. Taking your medications at regular times during the day and using common daily events to remind you to take your pills are useful strategies to help keep your medication plan on track. For example, you may place your morning dose in the bathroom so that when you are brushing your teeth in the morning you see and remember to take your pills. Because midday doses are particularly hard to remember, you will want to develop a way to link taking your medication with another well-established habit in your life such as eating lunch. With repeated practice, taking the lunchtime dose becomes as automatic as eating your meal.

One reason you may miss a dose is that you may forget to take your pills with you before you leave your home. Many patients cope with this by keeping a small supply of pills (enough for three days) in different places (for example, a separate container of pills in a desk drawer, luggage, or knapsack). Keeping back-up pills in your travel bags makes it that much harder to leave for a vacation or business trip without your pills.

It is also important that you communicate the importance of medication treatment to your family members. At times, family members may be unaware of the beneficial effects of the medication and may be frightened by the idea that you are taking medicine. Some well-meaning family members or friends may want you to just get better and may end up encouraging you to skip your treatment or to miss a clinic appointment. Family and friends often do this out of an understandable desire to see you as recovered or not really ill in the first place. Unfortunately, this seldom leads to any benefit and usually has the unfavorable effect of increasing your potential for worsening symptoms or a relapse.

To help prevent these outcomes and reduce negative pressures on you, we invite you to have your family members or other support persons read this chapter, as well as the rest of this book. We also believe that it would be beneficial for you to discuss with them how they can support you in keeping on schedule with your medications or your office visits.

Finally, remember to keep track of the amount of pills that you have left in your bottle. This way you can ask your doctor for refills or you can pick up your refills before you run out of medication. Remember that medications are a useful tool to help you maintain your mood within the range you want so that you can best pursue your life goals. These tools are only useful if you use them the right way.

Consistent Use of Your Medication

For many individuals, a combination of medications may be used to enhance mood stability. Once your mood stabilizes, there is often the temptation to discontinue medication and to believe that the disorder has been cured. Unfortunately, bipolar disorder is a lifelong condition, one that requires ongoing treatment. We use the analogy of a seatbelt to help underscore the importance of this point. As you know, a seatbelt is a protective device designed to prevent injury in the case of a car accident. Hopefully, that accident never happens, but if it does, you are prepared. In a similar way, taking medications for bipolar disorder protects you from depression and mania. Even when your symptoms feel completely under control, it is important to take your medications regularly.

> *Even when your symptoms feel completely under control, it is important to take your medications regularly.*

At times, you may miss some of the highs that go with a hypomanic mood. However, remember that the goal of taking the pills is to keep you in control of your life. Manic episodes take away that control and the ability for you to plan your life the way you want. Be careful of sacrificing your life goals for a desire to feel high. First, use medications to help you stay in control, and then figure out how to make life as fun and fulfilling as possible.

The self-guided care box on page 30 is designed to provide you with opportunities to think through and clarify your goals for using medications as tools to help control your bipolar disorder. Writing out your responses will help you better articulate your reasons and will also provide you with a written record for review at a later time.

Coping with Medication Side Effects

Medication side effects are difficult, but you are not alone with this struggle. If you are experiencing bothersome side effects, schedule a meeting with your psychiatrist or therapist to discuss ways of coping with these symptoms. In response to your side effects, you and your physician may determine that it is necessary to discontinue a particular medication. Most often, adjusting the dose or the time the medication is taken makes it possible to tolerate the medicine long enough to get whatever benefit it has to offer. Side effects tend to be most difficult just after a medication is added, but tend to gradually subside over time. However, sometimes side effects will

Self-Guided Care: Motivation for Medication Use

I wish to use medications regularly for my benefit, to help return my moods to the normal range, or to help protect me against a future mood episode. When I am feeling better, I may have some urges to quit my medications. At those times, it will be important for me to remember why I want to continue my medications. Medication is used to protect me against the following effects of depression and mania.

Manic symptoms and life-consequences I want to avoid:

1. _____

2. _____

3. _____

Depression symptoms and life-consequences I want to avoid:

1. _____

2. _____

3. _____

A few reminders I want to use to help me stay motivated for medication use:

1. _____

2. _____

3. _____

remain bothersome to you and the best course of action may be to continue the medication despite the side effects. In that case, you and your treatment team may add coping skills to reduce the impact of these side effects on your life.

The most important thing to remember is to stay in treatment and to discuss your concerns with your doctor when you have side effects. It is important that you do not let the side effects deter you from taking your medication. Instead, be active. Work with your treatment team to solve side-effect problems. Time spent finding the medication that works for you is time well spent.

> *Work with your treatment team to solve side-effect problems.*

Medication Monitoring

Monitoring your medication is a good idea to help ensure that you continue to take your medications as prescribed. This is part of making sure that you use the tools that you and your treatment team have selected in the best manner. Chapter 12 provides a form for monitoring your moods and activities to maximize your daily control over your disorder. This form also includes a place to record your use of medications. Research has found that even this simple extra attention to monitoring pill taking helps people stay on track with their daily use of medication. With a little practice at linking pill taking to daily routines, and regular monitoring of moods and medication use, you can maximize the value that medications can have in helping control your bipolar disorder.

Medications and Pregnancy

Women with bipolar disorder who want to have children should work very closely with family support and health care providers when thinking about conceiving. Careful planning and being well-informed are the keys to successful management of bipolar illness during and after pregnancy. Careful planning can help you best manage bipolar disorder by minimizing symptoms and avoiding risks to your unborn child. First, it is important to never stop taking medications before talking with your prescribing doctor. You also shouldn't make sudden changes to your medication as you consider conception or during pregnancy. Such changes might lead to major side effects, risks to the fetus, and increase your risk for a mood episode. Second, more information than ever is available on medications used to treat bipolar disorder and their impact on the fetus. Contact and carefully plan with your physician which medications provide you with the best balance of mood stabilization and safety for your baby during pregnancy. This planning should include discussions with your clinician prior to initiating conception, discussions during the course of pregnancy, and planning for the postpartum and nursing phases of having a child.

5

Psychotherapy for Bipolar Disorder

This book is designed to provide you and members of your support network with basic information about bipolar disorder and its management. Each of the chapters focuses on a different element of functioning that may influence the course of bipolar disorder. These topic areas—information about the disorder, medication use and compliance, stress and schedule management, thinking biases, relationships, communication skills, problem solving, and construction of a treatment contract—are the same topic areas that typically receive attention in psychotherapy. Psychotherapy provides a chance to get more help with these or other topics that are relevant for individuals with bipolar disorder.

When you choose psychotherapy, it is important to find a therapist who is knowledgeable about bipolar disorder and with whom you are comfortable talking. A good therapist can be a crucial addition to your treatment team.

> *A good therapist can be a crucial addition to your treatment team.*

When choosing a therapist, you and your family need to be smart shoppers. Talk with the therapist about his or her approach to treating bipolar disorder, including the therapist's expectations regarding the length of treatment and when you should first expect to see benefits. Also ask for the therapist's expectations of you and how you can make the best use of psychotherapy.

Psychotherapy can play an important role in helping you manage bipolar disorder. At any time you may supplement the information and strategies introduced in this book with the more specific help that can be provided by a therapist. In all cases, remember that you are the primary consumer of treatment. Always act as an informed caregiver to yourself and pull together a treatment team that can provide you with the best benefit.

Specific Psychotherapies for Bipolar Disorder

The past decade has brought welcome research attention to how psychotherapy can help in the management of bipolar disorder. To date, three types of psychotherapy have received prominent attention in research studies: family-focused therapy, interpersonal psychotherapy, and cognitive-behavior therapy. We want you to know the brand name of these therapies because they may help you identify therapists who have specialized in the treatment of bipolar disorder and who have adopted a treatment style that has been examined by research. However, it is also important to know that these three types of psychotherapy share many of the same elements of treatment. That is, even though the originators of these treatments come from different theoretical traditions, the elements of treatment they emphasize are very similar. We find this comforting and believe it reflects a shared understanding of what is important for the management of bipolar disorder.

Family focused therapy is oriented toward seeing the individual with bipolar disorder together with her or his family. It emphasizes education about the nature of the disorder combined with active work in providing better communication patterns within the family and in developing an active problem-solving style for the challenges brought by bipolar disorder. Individuals and family members in treatment can expect direct attention to the mood episodes that define the disorder, but also attention to how everyday emotions are perceived and handled within the family, with a goal of promoting understanding, good communication, and wellbeing for all family members. A focus on education and communication patterns is also at the heart of *interpersonal psychotherapy* (IPT), a therapy that directs attention to the interpersonal conflicts and role challenges that are associated with mood disorders. The focused approach on interpersonal issues helps ensure a problem-focused way to resolve some of these issues. For the management of bipolar disorder, this treatment also explicitly includes a focus on managing activities and sleep/wake cycles to try to reduce the ways in which these cycles affect mood episodes. *Cognitive-behavior therapy* (CBT) also includes this focus on managing activity levels in relation to long-term goals, enhancing communication and problem solving, enhancing stress management, and helping manage the negative or overpositive thinking patterns that play a role in maintaining or exacerbating mood episodes. For all of these treatments, there is also attention to the symptoms that may signal that a mood episode is likely, with the therapist working with the individual with bipolar disorder to intervene early to reduce the likelihood of a full episode.

All of these types of treatments share the idea that therapy should be an active process for both the therapist and the patient. These are not therapies where you do all the talking and receive no guidance. In each of these therapies, the therapist is there to share her or his knowledge of the disorder and practical strategies for managing mood episodes and reducing the impact of bipolar disorder on your life and your goals. For this reason, we want you to be very active in talking with a potential new therapist about his or her approach and what can be expected from therapy. Research has provided some guidance on the elements of therapy that can be helpful in changing the course of the disorder, and we want you to be active in trying to seek out these elements of treatment and finding a therapist with whom you feel comfortable and confident.

Bipolar Disorder in Adolescents and Children

Although there has been a lot of controversy about this diagnosis in children, there is increasing evidence that bipolar disorder can affect children. It is estimated that 1%–1.5% of children have bipolar disorder, and among adults with the disorder, one-third to one-half report that their mood episodes began during childhood or adolescence. The initial episode in children and adolescents is often depression, with onset of mood episodes occurring most frequently in later childhood or early adolescence, although anxiety and other emotional disturbances may be present much earlier. Because bipolar disorder is a genetic illness, the risks for bipolar disorder increase if family members have the disorder, particularly if both parents have the disorder (and may exceed a 50:50 chance).

How Does Bipolar Disorder Present in Children?

As with adults, children and adolescents with bipolar disorder can experience symptoms of mania, hypomania, and depression. However, there are important differences among adults and children and adolescents in the types of symptoms that are characteristic of mood episodes. For example, youth with bipolar disorder are more likely to have a form of the disorder that is chronic and rapid-cycling, with frequent, rapidly shifting episodes (sometimes even within the same day), and mixed episodes (with symptoms of both depression and mania). Youth are also more likely to present as extremely irritable with explosive outbursts.

During periods of depression, children can appear cranky, sad, whiny, and clingy. As with adults, they may have decreased energy and decreased interest in activities (some parents describe that their child is more like a "couch potato" than usual). The child may see herself or himself negatively (describe themselves as stupid, bad, or ugly), feel negatively about their lives and their future (e.g., "things never work out for me"), have difficulty concentrating or making decisions, and be restless or physically slowed down. Children and adolescents may also have difficulty sleeping or may sleep more than usual and experience changes in their appetite. It is important to note that youth, even young children, can experience suicidal thoughts (e.g., "I wish I was dead"; "I wish I'd never been born"), as well as suicidal impulses and behaviors. If a child is reporting any of these thoughts and feelings, it is important to take them seriously and have them quickly evaluated by a professional.

> *Even young children can experience suicidal thoughts, impulses, and behaviors.*

During periods of mania, children can appear very giddy, silly, high, and/or they may be extremely irritable and explosive. When irritable, they may have intense, long-lasting rages, which can be provoked by seemingly minor issues (or sometimes seem to come out of the blue). As in adult forms of the illness, children may display grandiosity (for example, thinking that they can fly; that they are the same as an adult), physical restlessness, and racing thoughts. They may talk very quickly, be more active (for example, doing more with friends, starting many new projects), and (less typically) require less sleep than usual. Children and adolescents may also behave in an impulsive or risky manner. Children and adolescents may be daredevils, and may display increased interest in sexual matters. During rages, youth may become verbally or physically aggressive, damage property, and appear out of control. More rarely, youth may experience psychotic symptoms, such as hearing voices, or having intense, unusual and unrealistic beliefs, called delusions.

Comorbidity

Youth with bipolar disorder often have other disorders as well. Recent research suggests that 60% or more have attention-deficit-hyperactivity disorder (ADHD). Many children with bipolar disorder also have other behavioral problems such as oppositional-defiant disorder (ODD) or conduct disorder. A significant percentage of children with bipolar disorder also have problems with anxiety, including excessive anxiety about being separated from parents, social anxiety, and excessive worry. These children may also be more likely to have learning or developmental disabilities.

What Is the Course of the Illness in Children?

At this time, the long-term course of bipolar disorder in children has not yet been determined. However, many adults with bipolar disorder report that their symptoms started in childhood or adolescence, suggesting that the disorder is continuous across development. The few studies that have followed children with bipolar disorder over time suggest that the disorder often follows a waxing and waning course. For example, recent short-term follow-up studies suggest that bipolar disorder in youth tends to be chronic, with long episodes and a high risk for relapse after remission.

How Does Bipolar Disorder Impact Children?

Children with bipolar disorder often experience difficulty at home, at school, and/or with peers. Some children with bipolar disorder function well at school but can be very disruptive at home. Because the child's moods and behaviors can be unpredictable, family members may feel stressed and anxious about the child's symptoms. For example, parents will sometimes report that they are walking on eggshells to avoid triggering an emotional explosion. There may also be significant conflict in the family associated with the child's oppositionality, aggression, and emotional instability. Children with bipolar disorder also may often exhibit anger and aggression toward their siblings and family pets.

Children with bipolar disorder can display a range of functioning at school. Some children do very well academically, socially, and emotionally in the structured setting of school. Some children experience minor difficulties. However, some children experience significant difficulty at school. They may be unable to remain focused and attentive, may feel groggy or tired because of medication, or have trouble sitting still during classes. They may also have difficulty regularly attending school or getting to school on time because of an inability to rouse in the morning. Many children and adolescents may feel exhausted or burnt out by the end of the school day, making it extremely difficult to complete homework assignments. Children may also exhibit behavioral problems at school and behave in a noncompliant or aggressive manner toward school staff. Taken together, these problems may significantly interfere with their ability to master academic material, successfully complete schoolwork, and enjoy school.

The transition from high school to college may be challenging for older adolescents with bipolar disorder. They may feel overwhelmed by the increased demands for independence and self-regulation. They may also become overwhelmed by the amount of schoolwork required. They may have trouble going to class regularly and completing work without the structure that they were used to in high school. Emotionally, they may struggle with the added responsibilities of becoming an adult (e.g., paying bills and managing their own time).

Youth with bipolar disorder may also experience difficulty with peer relationships, including social isolation, teasing, and frequent conflict with other children. If they exhibit impulsive or aggressive behaviors, they may have difficulty making or sustaining friendships. Children and adolescents may miss social cues or misinterpret the intentions of others (e.g., thinking that other children are being mean when they are not) and may feel very anxious about interacting with others. They may also feel emotionally overwhelmed by social demands and may avoid or withdraw from peers.

How Is Childhood Bipolar Disorder Treated?

The first step to treating this disorder is to obtain a thorough evaluation. The evaluation should be made by a child psychiatrist or child psychologist with expertise in assessing and diagnosing mood disorders in children. The evaluation typically includes speaking with the parent(s), as well as interviewing and observing the child. The evaluation will include a review of the child's current symptoms, a review of his or her history and development, questions about family history, previous treatments, and medical history. Additional forms of assessment such as neuropsychological or psychological testing may be helpful in clarifying other areas of difficulty, although these tests cannot diagnose bipolar disorder.

Medications

As with adult bipolar disorder, medications are central to treating bipolar disorder in children and adolescents. The medications that are used in youth are the same ones that are typically prescribed to adults, including mood stabilizers (e.g., Depakote and lithium), and atypical antipsychotics (e.g., Risperdal, Seroquel, and Zyprexa). Although less is known about the effects of these medications in youth, research suggests that they can be very helpful in reducing mood symptoms, decreasing aggression, and improving functioning.

Additional medications such as stimulants or antidepressants may also be prescribed to address other symptoms or disorders that the child is experiencing. However, these medications are not typically prescribed until the child is on a mood stabilizing treatment and is more stable because these medications can sometimes exacerbate or bring on symptoms of bipolar disorder.

Psychotherapy

Although little is known about the effectiveness of psychotherapy for childhood bipolar disorder, it may be useful (with older children or adolescents) in helping youth learn about their disorder, address issues of self-esteem, and address issues of functioning. A specific form of therapy called cognitive-behavior therapy (CBT) may be used to target distorted thinking patterns, develop coping skills, address anxiety, and improve social skills. Among adolescents, therapy may also address strategies for decreasing high-risk behaviors such as alcohol or substance use and abuse.

Family therapy can be an especially important component of treatment. Parents may benefit from learning different ways of interacting and parenting children with bipolar disorder. They may also benefit from learning strategies to help children manage their mood symptoms, address behavior problems, and decrease stress and conflict in the family. Recent research suggests that family conflict and stress can precipitate relapse of bipolar disorder in adults and adolescents, suggesting that decreasing these problems may be important in managing bipolar symptoms. In addition, it is important for parents to obtain support because it can often be very stressful and isolating to have a child who is experiencing this illness. Finally, siblings may benefit from the opportunity to learn about bipolar disorder and talk about their concerns.

School Supports for Children with Bipolar Disorder

Many children and adolescents with bipolar disorder may benefit from additional supports or accommodations at school. Because bipolar disorder is considered a disability under federal law, some children and adolescents with bipolar disorder may qualify for special education services and be eligible for an Individualized Education Plan (IEP). Alternatively, children may be eligible to receive accommodations under a Section 504 plan. Because it can be tricky to navigate the special education system, it is important for parents to educate themselves about their child's eligibility and the services that can be provided. Working closely with school psychologists or guidance counselors, teachers, special education personnel, or school administrators is critical in ensuring that the child receives the appropriate services. In some instances, it may be very helpful to talk with an educational consultant, educational advocate, or educational lawyer who has expertise in special educational plans and/or alternative school placements for youth with bipolar disorder.

Although it is crucial that an education plan be individualized to the needs of each child, some general accommodations that may be helpful for children with bipolar disorder include those used for other academic or emotional challenges.

- Reducing or eliminating homework demands. In some instances, it may also be possible to arrange for the child to work on homework during the school day.
- Access to a resource room for specific classes.
- Preferential seating in the classroom.
- A functional behavioral assessment and a behavioral program in the classroom.
- A program to increase communication between home and school (e.g., communication log).
- Specialized instruction for learning disabilities.

- Occupational or speech/language therapy.
- Maintaining a second set of textbooks at home.
- Reducing the number of classes taken or shortening the school day.
- A one-on-one or shared special education aide in the classroom.
- Allowing for extended time on tests.
- Reducing the need for handwriting assignments by using a keyboard or a scribe.
- A social skills group.
- In-school counseling.
- Identifying a point-person to whom the child can go and talk to if distressed or in crisis.
- Providing a quiet place where the child can calm down and relax.
- An extended school year (services over the summer).
- For children with more severe problems, placement in a separate therapeutic classroom within the school, alternative therapeutic day school, or residential program.

Planning Around College

It is important to know that, for children receiving special education services, services can be provided through the age of 21. Although there are differences between high schools and post-secondary programs in the services that they must provide, colleges will provide accommodations to enable the student with a disability to access the curriculum. In addition, many colleges offer more extensive supports for students with disabilities, and there are colleges and post-secondary programs around the country that have been specially designed for students with ADHD, learning disabilities, and/or emotional difficulties. More minor accommodations that may be helpful to students entering college include reducing the number of courses taken (in some instances, a college student with bipolar disorder may be considered a full-time student even with a reduced course load), maintaining as much structure as possible (e.g., seeking colleges with smaller class sizes or that mandate class attendance), and seeking designated quiet or "dry" dormitories (those that prohibit alcohol or drug use).

Helpful Parenting Strategies

Parenting a child with bipolar disorder can be a stressful and frustrating experience. First and foremost, it is important for parents to remember that they are not to blame for their child's difficult behaviors. It is also important to remember that these children are suffering from an illness that can get in the way of their behaving appropriately. Although their behavior in the moment can be quite outrageous, children often feel very remorseful or ashamed once the crisis has passed. In addition, the following general parenting strategies may be helpful.

- *Maintain structure and regularity in activities.* As with adults, children with bipolar disorder are vulnerable to disruptions in their schedules. They may benefit from a predictable schedule of activities that is not too hectic but avoids long periods of downtime. This can be particularly important during the weekends or vacation. Relaxing or soothing activities can also help a child during stressful periods or during particularly difficult times of day.
- *Keep a mood log.* A mood log or brief journal will help you identify patterns in your child's moods, identify potential triggers, and become aware of early warning signs of mood episodes.
- *Plan ahead.* As much as possible, avoid unnecessary situations that are likely to trigger meltdowns. If a difficult situation is unavoidable, prepare for it in advance (in collaboration with your child if they are old enough to do so).
- *Decrease family conflict.* It is important to decrease overall family conflict and stress because these can destabilize the moods of both children and adults with bipolar disorder. Pick and choose your battles carefully before imposing a limit. Be consistent in

the limits you set, and enforce them in a firm but nonaggressive and nonconfrontational manner. If possible, involve your child in solving issues to teach him or her problem-solving skills. Remember that parents serve as models for child behavior, so, as much as possible, work to provide your child with frequent examples of step-by-step problem solving and conflict resolution (family therapy may help to a great degree here). If arguments become aggressive, implement strategies to de-escalate tension (e.g., a family time-out until all parties have calmed down). If parents disagree about how to handle a problem, avoid arguing or discussing this in front of your child.

- *Remember your child's strengths.* Encourage your child to channel their energies into appropriate tasks and activities. Remember to praise appropriate behaviors, and point out talents and positive traits.

- *Be aware of stressful events outside the home.* Stay in close contact with the school because stressors at school or with peers can lead to meltdowns at home. Talk with your child about these stressful events and ways of managing them.

- *Facilitate transitions.* Because transitions (including daily transitions) can be particularly difficult, provide plenty of warning for upcoming transitions (ranging from larger transitions such as school onset and offset and vacations to nightly bedtime) provide sufficient time for the child to transition at their speed, limit the number of unnecessary steps during transitions, and try to keep routines as consistent as possible.

- *Monitor your teenager's behavior.* Because teens with bipolar disorder are especially vulnerable to alcohol or drug abuse, as well as other risky behaviors, it is important that parents be aware of their peer relationships and behaviors outside the home. Also keep close tabs on internet, instant messenger (IM), and cell phone use because impulsive behaviors can get your teen into trouble.

- *Have a crisis plan in place.* If your child can become violent or suicidal, develop an emergency plan ahead of time (be sure to include his or her treatment providers in this plan). Know which hospital you may want to use for an inpatient stay for you child, and know the steps needed for admission (see Chapter 8). At crisis times, make sure that dangerous items (e.g., knives and medications) are out of the reach of children. Maintain the safety of siblings and pets. Avoid confrontations in potentially dangerous situations (such as while driving in the car).

- *Be aware of unrealistic expectations.* It may be tempting to compare your child to other children (or his or her siblings). However, remember that just because you or others feel that a child should be able to do something does not mean that they can. Understand your child's special needs and work with them to achieve what they can at their own pace. Set intermediate goals that the child can work towards, step-by-step.

- *Take care of yourself.* Parenting a bipolar child or adolescent can be exhausting, stressful, and isolating. It is crucial that parents take time out for themselves to "recharge their batteries." Obtain support from family or others who understand what it is like to have a child with bipolar disorder. Consider additional resources in the community, including therapy, after-school programs, or support groups.

Part II

Managing Your Disorder

7

Stress and Schedule Management

Role of Stress in Bipolar Disorder Episodes

Stressful situations (such as interpersonal conflicts or financial set-backs) can increase the likelihood of a depressive or manic episode. Sometimes even positive life events, such as getting married or starting a new job, can lead to stress. This chapter presents techniques that can help you cope with stress. As you read, you will find some techniques more interesting than others. Select techniques you find of interest and include them in your treatment contract, which you will create later on (see Chapter 13).

Managing Your Sleeping Patterns

Research has shown that changes in your normal sleep cycle increase the risk of episodes of mania or depression. Because you cannot always avoid stress, maintaining regular sleep patterns can help stabilize your mood.

The first step in using sleep as a buffer against episodes of depression and mania is to wake up and go to bed at the same times, even on weekends.

Maintaining regular sleep patterns can help stabilize your mood.

Although it may be tempting to stay up later and sleep in on weekends, this change in sleep may increase the chance of depression or mania. The bottom line is—the more consistent you are in maintaining a sleep schedule, the better your chances are of keeping your mood stable. This strategy does not have to be carried out in an all-or-nothing fashion. If you find it difficult to keep to a regular sleep schedule, you may simply choose to use a more defined schedule during stressful times.

If you are having difficulty sleeping, it may be helpful to pay attention to the following sleep tips.

- *Keep stress out of the bedroom.* Discussing your concerns about your life or family or doing work-like activities (e.g., paying bills and reading documents for work) should not take place in your bed or in the bedroom. Save the bedroom for bed activities. Worry or work at a desk, not in bed.
- *Use muscle relaxation techniques in bed.* Relaxation tapes may help you relax and feel even more comfortable in bed. Remember the goal is not to go to sleep but to become very comfortable in bed so that sleep comes naturally. Commercially available relaxation tapes may help with this process.
- *Never compete to get to sleep.* If you find that you are having difficulty sleeping, do not try harder. Trying hard to get to sleep often has the opposite effect; it wakes a person up with feelings of frustration and anger. Instead, try to *enjoy being in bed and*

resting, even if sleep does not come. Direct your attention to how comfortable you can be in bed (how the pillow feels or how good it feels to lie down and stretch), how relaxed your muscles feel, and how you can let your thoughts drift. In other words, let yourself be very passive about sleep. *Your job is to be comfortable in bed and let sleep come to you.*

- *Give yourself time to unwind before sleep.* Make sure the last hour of activity before bedtime is relatively passive. Do not pay bills, do not work out life problems, and do not plan your workday, save these activities for earlier in the day when you are fresher. Before sleep, choose activities that are pleasant and take very little effort (e.g., television, reading, talking). Go to bed only after you have had a chance to unwind and feel more like sleeping.

- *Use a regular daytime cycle to help with nighttime sleep.* Avoid taking naps during the day. Use regular exercise (at least three hours before bedtime) to help increase sleep and induce normal fatigue. Reduce caffeine use (certainly eliminate caffeine use after noon), and be wary of drinking alcohol or smoking within several hours of bedtime. One way to establish a regular time for falling asleep is to have a regular time for waking up. Setting your alarm clock to a reasonable time and maintaining it throughout the week will eventually be helpful in stabilizing your sleep time.

- *Adjust sleep cycle before travel.* Traveling across time zones also has the potential to disrupt regular sleep patterns. Whenever possible, gradually adjust your sleep cycle over the course of several days to match that of the new time zone. However, if your travel will be brief, as in a business trip, it might be better to keep to your regular schedule and not switch to the new time zone.

Keeping a Regular Schedule

Changes in your mood have the potential to disrupt your schedule of daily activity. For example, when you are depressed, it may be difficult to get out of bed, and you may feel less motivated to pursue a busy schedule of activities. Alternatively, when your mood is elevated, you may feel more energized and take on more activities or projects than usual. Structuring a regular pattern of activities and sticking to it can help stabilize your mood. By adopting a regular pattern of exercise, eating, work, and social interaction, you can provide external cues that help keep your biological clock on the correct time. You may think of yourself working with this technique much like a piano player uses a metronome to keep the correct rhythm. This pattern should include a balance of activities that are pleasurable and that lead to a sense of accomplishment.

In addition to acting as a buffer against stress, paying attention to your regular schedule of activities also may provide you with clues to the beginning of a mood episode. That is, when you notice that your patterns of activities are changing, it is a signal to you that a mood episode may be starting. This should serve as a reminder to speak with your doctor, therapist, or support system and to take measures to avoid a full-blown episode of mania or depression.

Keeping an activity chart can help you structure a personalized weekly pattern of activities that work for you. An activity chart also provides you with a way to help ensure that you stay involved in regular activities that you value. The first step in making an activity chart is to think about some of the enjoyable activities that you used to do or want to do. Once you identify these activities, write them in the box provided.

Activity Charting

An activity chart can be used to track and stabilize work and leisure activities.

An activity chart can be used to track and stabilize work and leisure activities. Using the chart provided, write in regular activities (such as your workday, regular appointments, and

Self-Guided Care: Valued Activities

Exercise

_____

_____

_____

Social Activities

_____

_____

_____

Relationship Activities

_____

_____

_____

Movies, Theater, and Recreation

_____

_____

_____

Hobbies

_____

_____

_____

Work-Related Activities

_____

_____

_____

other commitments). Then, write in regular activities that you want to engage in during the week to provide some pleasant moments. For example, make sure that you become involved in exercise, or a hobby, a favorite television show, or a movie on a Wednesday evening so that the entire week is less stressful. As you take time to ensure regular involvement in stress-buffering activities, please consider the list of potentially pleasurable activities provided here. The value of this list is that it encourages you to consider a range of regular activities that serve as pleasant events in your life as well as a buffer against stress. Regular exercise in particular has been shown to have a wide range of mental health benefits that include a decrease in anxiety, stress, and most notably, reduced depression. Accordingly, the activity list includes a variety of exercise-based activities that may offer you direct mood benefits.

When considering starting or changing your exercise routine, please plan an appropriate starting program relative to your level of fitness. Also, review your exercise plan with your physician so that you have her or his recommendations for the intensity of any new exercise regimen. In every case, it is important to start slowly and work up in intensity during weeks of exercise, rather than face the soreness and injury of an overenthusiastic start to a new exercise program.

Make sure your new pleasurable activities do not cut into your sleep time. Remember that a regular schedule can help you have more fun and less stress and at the same time help protect you from mood episodes.

Table 7.1 Activity Chart

	Morning	Midday	Afternoon	Evening
Monday				
Tuesday				
Wednesday				
Thursday				
Friday				
Saturday				
Sunday				

Self-Guided Care: Activity for Mood Stabilization

The following list is designed to stimulate ideas for activities that may improve your weekly pleasure as well as provide stress-buffering effects. In considering the list, think of the *variations on themes* that may make an activity especially rewarding. For example, going swimming at a local pond instead of the local pool or grilling in a local park instead of your backyard may make your activity more memorable. Likewise, little things added to a regular activity—buying your favorite childhood candy at the movie theater or fixing a cup of hot chocolate to drink while reading a novel—transform an experience by evoking past pleasant memories.

Because the mood-promoting effects of exercise are powerful, the list begins with these activities. Any level of exercise is a good start, but over time, for exercise to have its desired effect on mood, you should exercise for 30 minutes a day, three days per week. When you go through the list, check off those activities of most interest to you.

- Take daily walks for pleasure
- Jog (park, track, gym)
- Rollerblade
- Ride a bicycle
- Go swimming
- Go windsurfing
- Try sailing
- Paddle a canoe or kayak
- Go fishing in a local stream or pond
- Go skiing
- Go ice skating
- Play tennis
- Kick around a soccer ball
- Join a softball league
- Play volleyball

- Shoot baskets with a friend
- Set up a racquetball date
- Call two friends and go bowling
- Play with a frisbee
- Take a kid to mini golf
- Start a program of weight lifting
- Take a yoga class
- Go to an indoor rock climbing center—take a lesson
- Build a snow fort and have a snowball fight
- Walk in the snow and listen to your footsteps
- Catch snowflakes in your mouth
- Sign up for a sculpting class
- Bake a cake
- Draw
- Paint (oils, acrylics, watercolor)
- Climb a tree
- Go for an evening drive
- Go to a drive-in movie
- See a movie
- Volunteer to work at a soup kitchen
- Join a museum Friday night event
- Write a letter to a friend
- Sing a song
- Play a musical instrument
- Take an art class
- Walk a dog
- Volunteer to walk dogs for a local animal shelter
- Play with children
- Visit a pet shop and look at the animals
- Sit in the sun
- Read in a rocking chair
- Sit on a porch swing
- Go for a hike

- Learn to knit
- Do a crossword puzzle (every day for a week)
- Go out for an ice cream sundae
- Rent a garden plot at a local farm or community space
- Grill dinner in the backyard
- Take a bath at night with candles around the tub
- Read the newspaper in a coffee shop
- Schedule a kissing-only date with your romantic partner
- Order hot chocolate in a restaurant
- Buy flowers for the house
- Get a massage
- Reread a book you read in high school or college
- Bake cookies for a neighbor
- Have a garage sale (perhaps with a neighbor)
- Wear purple
- Start a program of daily morning sit-ups or push-ups
- Get an atlas and look up a country you don't know about
- Buy a spool of wire and make a sculpture
- Go to an art museum and find one piece you really like
- Buy a magazine on a topic you know nothing about
- Polish all of your shoes
- Buy a new plant
- Clean out a closet
- Write a letter to the editor of the local newspaper
- Repaint a table or a shelf
- Go to a diner for breakfast
- Devote a meal to cooking red, white, and blue foods
- Plan an affordable three-day vacation
- Start a collection of heart-shaped rocks
- Find your top three favorite videos on YouTube and share them with a friend
- Woodworking—build a table or a chair
- Burn a CD of your favorite movie music

- Take a dance class
- Learn to fold dollar bills into origami creatures
- Soak your feet in warm water
- Learn to juggle
- Clean and polish the inside of your car
- Go to a concert
- Meditate
- Organize a weekly game of cribbage or bridge
- Look at a map
- Plan a drive in the country
- Sew some napkins
- Make a pizza and bake it
- Buy a cookbook and make three new meals
- Read a novel
- Listen to your favorite song from high school...really loudly
- Rent a video, make popcorn, and invite friends over

Schedule a Time for Solving Problems

To help keep worry out of your life, establish one or two specific times in your weekly schedule for dealing with life issues. Focusing on life issues as a regular part of the week helps ensure that life's problems do not become overwhelming. Having a regular time to focus on issues may also help prevent worrying on a daily basis. Worry, unlike problem solving, is not useful. It taxes your energy, time, and emotions. Worry is characterized by negative thoughts such as "It will be awful if _____ happens!" You may not even know whether it really will be awful if _____ happens, but the thought of something awful occurring is usually enough to increase your anxiety. If you usually spend a lot of time worrying, you will spend less time thinking about solutions.

Problem solving is a step-by-step approach to examine whether anything more effective can be done to make your life better. In order to make problem-solving strategies useful, we recommend that you devote at least one hour each week to evaluating your life issues using the following format. Go through this guided format carefully and slowly, writing as you go. It is designed to help you approach problem solving in a freer manner by separating the process of *coming up with options* from the process of *evaluating* and then *selecting* from these problem-solving options This method does not guarantee that you will come up with a good solution. It does, however, make sure that you think about the problem effectively and take the time to examine the best solutions you can think of on any given day. To help with you the problem-solving process, we have provided an example here.

Self-Guided Care: Problem Solving

What is the problem:

Arguments with my wife about money

Why does this problem bother me (what are the specific features that bother me):

I always end up being the "heavy"

I want a better sense of control over our finances

Is this a realistic problem (e.g., what do I really think is going to happen, and what part of this problem do I think is just worry)?

Yes, we really do argue quite often about money

How can I rewrite the problem clearly, so that it helps me think about a solution? Write in a clear restatement of the problem:

My wife and I don't plan how to spend money, then are surprised by what each of us has spent, which leads to an argument

Now that I have the problem clearly in mind, what are potential solutions to this problem? To generate solutions, I want to think about as

---

many possible solutions as you can (without thinking why they are good or bad, and without choosing an option at this point). What advice might a good friend give? If a friend had this problem, what advice would I give? Potential options:

1. *Don't do anything differently*

2. *Set up a weekly meeting with my wife where we can discuss our finances and budgets*

3. *Open separate bank accounts*

4. *Use a notebook to track expenses and review with one another on a weekly basis*

5. *Assign a small amount of money as "free use" money and use a stricter budget for managing the rest*

Now rate each potential option. For each option rate the good and bad aspects of the proposed solution. Do not select an option until each is rated.

Good things about each solution	Bad things about each solution
I. *No effort required*	*Nothing is resolved and things may get worse*
2. *Gives us a chance to talk openly about finances and make money issues more clear*	*I may end up hating the meetings and fighting with my wife*
3. *Gives each of us a sense of freedom*	*I would feel like we aren't partners and it would be really hard to divide the money*
4. *Makes each of us accountable, makes sure we talk to each other about money, shows us where our money is going*	*We may fight during the meeting*

5. *Like option 3, this gives us more freedom*   *The amount of "free use" money will likely change from month to month, and shouldn't we be buying things together?*

Given this evaluation, which solution seems best?

Options 2 and 4 seem like the best solutions. Tracking our finances and meeting weekly seems to be a good way to start changing the situation.

Do you want to apply this solution, or is more time or more information needed to solve this problem?

Yes, I think we can start with this solution. I really want to change things and break the pattern of arguing over money.

Self-Guided Care: Problem Solving Schedule

My regular problem-solving times will be:

_____ (time) on _____ (day of the week) and/or

_____ (time) on _____ (day of the week).

Self-Guided Care: Problem Solving

What is the problem:

_____

Why does this problem bother me (what are the specific features that bother me):

_____

_____

_____

Is this a realistic problem (e.g., what do I really think is going to happen, and what part of this problem do I think is just worry)?

_____

How can I rewrite the problem clearly, so that it helps me think about a solution? Write in a clear restatement of the problem:

_____

_____

Now that I have the problem clearly in mind, what are potential solutions to this problem? To generate solutions, I want to think about as many possible solutions as possible (without thinking why they are good or bad, and without choosing an option at this point). What advice might a good friend give? If a friend had this problem, what advice would I give? Potential options:

_____

_____

_____

_____

_____

_____

Now rate each potential option. For each option rate the good and bad aspects of the proposed solution. Do not select an option until each is rated.

Good things about each solution   Bad things about each solution

1.

2.

3.

4.

5.

6.

Given this evaluation, which solution seems best?

_____

Do you want to apply this solution, or is more time or more information needed to solve this problem?

_____

Avoiding Destructive Activities: Control over Substance Abuse

Drug and alcohol use represents a special risk for people with bipolar disorder. Using alcohol or drugs does not allow medications to work as well and causes people to forget to take them. It also is linked with a greater number of hospitalizations. In particular, stimulants (e.g., cocaine or speed) are known to trigger mood episodes in people with bipolar disorder, and using drugs like PCP, angel dust, or ketamine (special K) may trigger psychotic episodes. Carefully consider whether you should drink alcohol, especially during periods when your mood is poor. In short, it pays to limit alcohol and drug use. For that reason, we recommend every treatment plan start with a 30-day period of complete abstinence from alcohol and recreational drugs. This will provide you and your treatment providers a chance to evaluate the role these substances play in your life. Use other pleasant events (see previous list) to increase your enjoyment, and keep your treatment team aware of any substances that you use. Your doctor and therapist will provide additional strategies if necessary to help you manage substance use. Remember that you are a core member of your treatment team; make sure you keep the rest of your treatment team informed about triggers for your mood episodes.

> *If you have bipolar disorder, it pays to limit your drug and alcohol use.*

Attention to Thinking Biases

Thinking Biases

The way that you think about an event or situation influences both your mood and behavior. For example, when you are depressed, you are more likely to think about a negative event in a more pessimistic way. This type of thinking or *cognitive style* can worsen a depressed mood, increase feelings of hopelessness, and decrease useful problem solving. This type of cognitive style is like looking at the world through darkly colored glasses that distort and darken reality in a negative way. The following are examples of cognitive distortions that are associated with depression.

- Black or White Thinking. This type of thinking involves seeing events in terms of extreme categories. Things that happen are either *right or wrong, wonderful or awful, success or failure,* or *black or white,* without any gray or middle ground. This can also be referred to as all-or-nothing thinking.
- Personalization. This type of cognitive error involves seeing yourself as the cause of some negative event or situation without having any evidence to support this conclusion. For example, a friend cancels a lunch date and you assume that you must have done something to offend her.

During periods of depression, we would like you to be especially aware of overly critical evaluations of yourself ("I blew it," "I am no good," "It never works out for me," "Look at me, I am . . . ") or of your future ("It won't work out," "there is no point"). During periods of depression, these thoughts tend to feel true (they are negative thoughts and they go with a negative mood state), but it is important to remember that thoughts in this form are extreme and do not do anything to guide you toward effective action. In considering the following sections, we would like you to keep in mind that your thoughts are only useful when they guide you effectively. If your thoughts are overly negative, overly positive, or overly critical, then they just can't have a role in helping you be more effective. We would like you to get to know the thoughts in the following sections so that you can be ready to ignore them or try to substitute them with more effective self-coaching when they occur. The thoughts share in common the tendency toward global and overarching statements, rather than focusing on a more reasoned evaluation of the situation or issue at hand. More effective coaching might include statements that not only acknowledge a problem but also suggest a course of action rather than global criticism (e.g., the thoughts, "Next time I need to approach this more carefully," "I should stop and plan," "I might need more practice to do this as effectively as I want," are all fair ways to coach yourself around a disappointment). Compare these thoughts with the motivation and esteem-sapping dysfunctional thoughts that follow.

- It is useless
- There is no point
- I will blow it anyway
- It will be just like last time when it did not go well
- I always fail

- I am no good
- I am different and flawed
- I should be different
- I should be better
- Look at me; I am not as good/happy/effective/bright/pretty as others

In being aware of negative thoughts, notice the presence of loaded words. These are words or phrases that are not accurate but evoke lots of emotion. Words such as *failed* or *disaster* can make any situation or event seem more dire and depressing. We would like you to challenge such words ("what do I really mean by *disaster*; what about this situation really deserves that label?") so that you are reacting honestly to the situations at hand rather than overly emotional descriptions of the situation.

Hyperpositive Thinking

In contrast to depression, a hypomanic or manic mood brings with it feelings of overconfidence with your abilities, decisions, and ideas, and underestimations of the potential risks. New ideas may feel especially good, and friends and colleagues may seem too conservative or not open to good ideas or fun. Specific hyperpositive thoughts may include:

- This is a great idea; my thinking is better than ever!
- They (including my friends) are just trying to hold me back because they don't know how special I am.
- No one knows how to have fun anymore.
- People worry about rules too much; rules are for slow thinkers.
- I can do anything.
- My work is too important; I don't need sleep.
- I have never felt so sexy; I need to share myself with more partners.

These thoughts share the themes of overconfidence and the inability to accurately predict negative consequences. As a result, serious social, family, career, and financial complications may happen to you. Often these types of thinking patterns start gradually in a hypomanic phase and escalate as mania develops. These types of changes in thinking should serve as a signal to you that your mood might be getting too high. Early action has the potential of reducing negative consequences.

Getting an Accurate Perspective on Thoughts

Remember that thoughts, whether true or not, can have a powerful effect on emotions. However, thoughts are only helpful if they are accurate. Mood disorders change the accuracy of thoughts: in depression they tend to be too negative and in mania they tend to be too positive.

> *Thoughts are only helpful if they are accurate.*

To avoid being needlessly pushed around by inaccurate thoughts, it is important to treat thoughts as hypotheses, or guesses, about the world. Before accepting a thought as true, it is important to evaluate the thought to see whether it is truly helpful to you. Specifically, we encourage you to examine the evidence for and against a given thought and see if an alternative thought might offer a more accurate picture of reality. Remember that your thoughts will be influenced by your current mood. Don't let your moods push you into believing inaccurate thoughts.

If you have trouble sorting through your thoughts, it may be helpful to discuss your concerns with a trusted friend, family member, or therapist. In addition, the self-guided care box provided here may help you keep inaccurate thoughts from pushing your moods around.

Suicidal Thinking and Self Care

At times, symptoms of bipolar disorder may include feelings of hopelessness. During intense times when symptoms are at their worst, things may *feel* so hopeless that life doesn't seem worth living. These feelings might also include thoughts of wanting to harm oneself or commit suicide. Suicidal thoughts can be overwhelming and frightening

Self-Guided Care: Evaluation of Thoughts

Is there an event that you find bothersome?

Event _____

Write out the thoughts that occur to you about this event, and the moods that go with this thought.

(thoughts)   (moods)

_____   _____

_____   _____

_____   _____

_____   _____

What is the evidence for and against this thought? Does the thought just feel true, or is there actual evidence for this thought? Could this evidence support any other conclusions?

_____

_____

What evidence suggests this thought is true?

_____

_____

What evidence suggests this thought is false?

_____

_____

Are there alternative explanations of the event?

_____

_____

Given your evaluation of the evidence, is there a more accurate thought you want to substitute? _____

in their own right and may occur during both the depressive and manic phases of the disorder.

The most important thing to remember about suicidal thoughts and behaviors are that they are *symptoms of your illness* and just like other symptoms of bipolar disorder they can be treated. With help, the majority of people with bipolar disorder do feel better. A first step to managing the risk of suicide in bipolar illness is for both individuals with bipolar disorder and their families to be familiar with the warning signs of suicide. Some of these include:

> *Suicidal thoughts and behaviors are symptoms of your illness and they can be treated.*

- Talking about suicide or frequent talking or thinking about death
- Making comments about being hopeless, helpless, or worthless
- Saying things such as "It would be better if I wasn't here" or "I want out"
- Worsening depression
- Sudden changes in mood (e.g., being very sad to very calm)
- Voluntarily putting oneself in harm's way
- Putting affairs in order (e.g., organizing finances or giving away possessions to prepare for one's death)

If these warning signs emerge, we want you to take steps to protect yourself and your family by discussing these symptoms with your clinician. Again, suicidal thoughts are symptoms and they need to be reported to a qualified mental health professional so that you can get help. Depending on the severity of these thoughts, this help may include a brief hospital stay. Remember that the purpose of this stay is to protect you until you feel better. This is the most basic and crucial aspect of care—a person needs to be protected during periods of severe symptoms so that he or she has the chance to improve. We want you to take every step to provide this protection and to use your treatment team in this process.

One straightforward strategy that has been shown in research studies to enhance safety in situations where an individual may be at risk for self harm is to make the process of getting help *easy*. The simple step of having all relevant contact information handy has itself been shown to protect individuals from suicidal actions. We want you to create contact numbers and information on an index card, and then share this card with those who care about you. Store this card in an easy to find place (e.g., a drawer, inside a kitchen cabinet, in front of your personal phone book). On this card, record the names and phone numbers of your treatment providers as well as phone numbers for the local emergency room and the phone number for the admissions personnel for the hospital *where you would prefer to get help*. Another important strategy for minimizing the risk that you will harm yourself is to include a suicide prevention plan as part of your Treatment Contract (see Chapter 13). You can work with your clinician and support team to incorporate this important planning component into your treatment contract so that everyone involved learns the warning signs to watch for and actions to take if you feel that you are slipping into suicidal thoughts.

In addition to a plan, both the individual with bipolar disorder and his or her family should know what to do in case of an emergency.

- Call your clinician or make arrangements for emergency care right away if you feel suicidal
- Ask for help from friends or family members to stay safe until you can get help

Call 911 or other emergency services if you:

- Think you cannot stop from harming yourself
- Hear voices
- Want to commit suicide

In all cases, it is important to protect yourself until you are in a position to recover and feel better.

Relationships and
Communication Skills

Sharing This Chapter

This chapter has two goals. The first is to provide you with information about communication strategies. The second is to provide this information to your family members or friends who are living with you. Sharing this chapter with your family is crucial because bipolar disorder can be a stressor on the whole family and household stress (including conflicts between people) can influence the number of episodes of depression or mania that you experience. In short, it is beneficial to you and your family to improve communication skills at home, to minimize stress, and, hopefully, to reduce the likelihood of future mood episodes.

How Can My Family or Support System Help?

Your family or support system can play a crucial role in helping you cope with bipolar disorder. We encourage you and your support system to read this book in its entirety. It is particularly important for you to review the content of this chapter with your family or other support network.

Think of your family or other support network as part of your treatment team. You will need to decide with them how they can assist with your care. Make sure your support team understands the importance of your psychiatric care. You may want to review Chapter 3 with them to ensure that they understand the importance of your medication treatment. Likewise, reviewing the following sections may be especially important for improving communication between you and your family or support team.

Improving communication is one way to reduce stress at home and improve family relations. A tolerant and low-key atmosphere at home may be particularly important for reducing episodes of depression or mania. Of course, maintaining a low-key atmosphere can be very difficult. Patients and families often face a dilemma when confronting emotionally charged issues. Patients frequently complain that every strong emotion they have is attributed to bipolar disorder, while family members complain that the person is too reactive to emotional issues. Also, it may cause frustration when a member of your support system tries to avoid topics of discussion that he or she thinks are too intense for you. A helpful technique in this circumstance is the whisper rule. This requires a simple agreement that when anyone feels like a topic is getting hot, they can request the discussion be held in a whisper. If the rule is violated, the conversation is put off for a set period of time (e.g., two hours). Patients who use this technique often instruct their families to take their ability to follow the whisper rule as a sign that their mood state is normal and to consider times when they are unable to follow this rule as an indication of being ill.

> *Improving communication can reduce stress at home and improve family relationships.*

Communication Skills

For discussions between family members or members of a support network, it is useful to keep in mind a gardener's tip:

"It pays to water the flowers not the weeds."

This tip underscores the importance of paying attention to what is working in your relationships, not what is going wrong. To water the flowers in your relationships you need to make sure that your family members know when they have done something that pleases you (e.g., being considerate, helping at home, etc.). All too often, individuals focus on and express only negative feedback. They complain about what isn't working, and this negative attention may increase bad feelings and fail to solve problems.

Attending to solutions rather than problems is especially important when a family member has a mood disorder such as bipolar disorder. Problems must be solved, but criticism and other forms of negative feedback may do more to worsen negative moods than to help with the issues at hand. Instead, more effective forms of communication need to be adopted.

Family members often have the greatest power when they are approving of others. Use this power! Make sure that you let others know when they are on track. This includes giving verbal feedback ("You know, I really liked it when you..."), using a positive tone, making pleasant eye contact, and giving touches or hugs when others are doing things you appreciate. These are important strategies for individuals with bipolar disorder, and they are also crucial strategies for helping patients reduce negative emotions.

Effective Listening

All too frequently, arguments and bad feelings arise in relationships because of misunderstandings about what was being said. Each party jumps to conclusions, emotions escalate, and feelings of anger, frustration, or hopelessness may result. To avoid this scenario as much as possible, it is important to ensure that communication is clear. A message must be received before a second message is sent.

Effective listening refers to the skill of making sure that you accurately hear the speaker's message and accurately communicate to the speaker that you heard it. To be an effective listener it is important to try to understand what the speaker is actually saying. To do this, you need to keep your reactions or counter-arguments under control long enough to devote attention to the message. Your job is not to have a quick answer, but to show the person speaking that you have heard her or his message. Once a clear message has been received, then and only then should you consider reacting to the message.

> *To be an effective listener it is important to try to understand what the speaker is actually saying.*

The following outline includes the core steps of effective listening. Under the best of conditions, both you and your partner in conversations will agree to use these effective listening strategies. These strategies may slow down a conversation, but in turn may greatly reduce time that may have been spent in a hurtful argument.

- Give the speaker clear signs that you are attending to what he or she is saying. Look at him or her in the eyes and nod as you hear each point.
- Ask questions to clarify individual points. Your goal is not to debate an issue, but to understand the speaker's perspective.
- Verify that you have heard the speaker's issues correctly by repeating the core content to the speaker. If the speaker does not agree, do not debate what was said (e.g., "but you said..."); instead, devote attention to getting the message clear.
- Once the speaker and you agree on the message, then it is your turn to respond. When you respond, the goal is to explain your perspective while respecting your listener's perspective.

Self-Guided Care: Using Better Communication

To help you get what you want, it is important that you use language that is useful for your goals. Practice restating negative statements in ways in which you are more likely to get your partner's attention and action.

When you feel like saying:

"*I am sick of this! You always* _____!"

Instead you could say (be specific and offer solutions):

"I feel really upset when you _____. It really would be helpful if you could instead _____."

Requesting Changes in Behavior

Remember that your goal with requests is to achieve a change in behavior. Your job is not to punish or shame. Punishment and shame often intensify the negative emotions in the household, further sapping joy from everyone's interactions. If you are going to request a change, you want to do it in a way that gives your listener a chance to succeed.

Instead of using a critical statement (e.g., "You never help me with anything around the house"), use a positive request for change that directs your partner toward success (e.g., "It would mean a lot to me if you could help me with some of the chores around the house"). Rather than act like an authority, do your best to enlist the listener's problem solving efforts. For example, you may ask for help with chores around the house and then suggest that your partner join you in listing and dividing up some of the chores.

Finally, when negative feelings are expressed, it is important to express these feelings in a specific rather than a general way. Avoid terms such as "you always..." or "you never...." These terms often serve to push away the listener, decreasing the chance you will get what you want. Instead, approach your partner (or other listener) with respect, describe what is upsetting you in specific terms, and make specific recommendations about how your partner can help things go better next time.

None of these skills guarantee that any given discussion will not deteriorate into a frustrating argument. However, use of these skills should help decrease the amount of conflict and bad feelings in your relationships over time. It takes practice to use these skills well.

Communicating With Your Clinician

Communication problems can frequently arise between patients and their clinicians. Patients and doctors are frustrated when the time allotted for a scheduled appointment runs out and important issues are not addressed. Your clinician needs to record information about your symptoms and response to treatment at every visit. Increasing the quality and the amount of information you provide at each visit also improves the quality of care you receive. You can accomplish this in a time-efficient manner by using a daily mood chart to effectively communicate your level of symptoms. One such mood chart is provided in Chapter 12; take a look at this chapter, discuss with your clinician, and see whether this mood chart can be used to summarize information on symptoms for your sessions with your clinician. With symptom information nicely summarized on the mood chart, more time is available to spend on other topics of importance to you.

Managing Irritability and Anger

Feelings of irritability and anger are fundamental symptoms of bipolar disorder that can occur as part of hypomanic, manic, or depressive episodes. When anger and irritability emerge as part of (hypo)mania, they often occur with a sense of internal pressure, including a humming sense of urgency, burden, or sensitivity to comments or actions from others. At times, individuals with bipolar disorder describe these feelings as a need to look for a fight, almost like they are seeking an explanation for the emotional tone in their bodies ("Oh yeah, I knew there was a reason I was feeling angry, it is because he/she is . . . "). When you experience this type of irritable mood, you focus your attention on potential slights and errors. Once you notice a small infraction, all of the irritable emotion is set into play ("I am so sick of this, I am going to put a stop to this right now") and an unnecessary argument or a self-defeating outburst can result.

Irritability and anger also emerge as part of depressive episodes. For many individuals, depressive irritability is similar to the feeling of having a constant toothache; because of the constant backdrop of pain, there is the sense of not being able to cope with much more. Sounds seem louder and shrill, imperfect behavior from others feels more intolerable, problems seem more catastrophic, and requests from others feel more overwhelming. At times, urges to fight against these annoyances are intensified by an internal sense of agitation, an inability to sit still, where the next annoyance feels like the perfect target to communicate, "stop it, stop it, stop it!" Similar to the feelings in irritable hypomania, the angry outburst feels justified at the moment. But later, when a sense of perspective returns, the thought is frequently, "I can't believe I got so upset and acted that way."

Part of effectively coping with bipolar disorder involves becoming skilled with understanding and reducing the impact of irritability and anger. One strategy for coping with irritability is to consult with your psychiatric provider to see if a medication adjustment may help keep these emotions in check. It is also useful to see how well you can develop additional anger management skills to break the links between mood disturbances, irritability, and aggressive behavior. In preparing to consider these skills, it is important to remember that the goal of anger management is to maximize your own wellbeing. Efforts to control anger do not deny the annoyances or frustrations in life. Instead, efforts to control anger are directed at avoiding the additional mood problems and strained relationships that anger causes.

> *Good anger management skills can break the links between mood disturbances, irritability, and aggressive behavior.*

To achieve your goals of reducing anger and irritation, we suggest rehearsal of four related skills. These skills are aimed at reducing the emergence as well as the escalation of anger. Should these preventive efforts fail, they are also targeted at minimizing aggressive behavior once it is initiated. Together, these four principles are designed to help you reduce the cost of irritability and anger episodes to your mood and to your relationships and work goals:

1. Don't let poor thinking habits goad you into an angry outburst or argument.
2. You don't have to solve an irritation *right now.*

3. Beware of win/lose thinking.
4. Remember to selfishly value your life goals, even when angry.

The remaining sections provide information on putting these principles to use.

Poor Thinking Habits and Anger

Keep your thoughts from pushing you around. Especially when feeling irritated, we would like you to be able to quickly evaluate and defuse thoughts that may help magnify annoyances into anger. These magnifying thoughts are of two primary types. One type serves to bring past annoyances and frustrations forward into the present so that any minor annoyance is weighted with these old emotions. The result is that a minor annoyance gets linked with a long cascade of irritating patterns that *must be stopped now.* For the examples that follow, notice how these thoughts can amplify a minor irritation into a major issue. We want you to get to know these thoughts so that they can't ignite irritation into a major anger episode.

- This is just like last time
- I can't let her/him/them get away with this
- They are always doing this to me
- Enough is enough
- I can't let this happen again
- I am always being treated this way
- They always act this way

These thoughts act to make the issue at hand too important and make you feel like you need to take a stand *right now.* Intensity of emotion is increased in part by taking past frustrations and bringing them forward to the present moment. In effect, these thoughts work to goad you on toward a more explosive conflict.

A second way to intensify anger and lose perspective is to guess at the motives of others. By using the right kind of self-talk, you can make an annoyance seem more like a personal attack. Take a look at the thoughts that follow and notice the way in which they increase a sense of victimization and anger.

- They are messing with me
- I am sick and tired of being manipulated
- They don't respect me
- She/he is out to get me
- He/she is doing this on purpose
- He does not care how I feel
- She knows I hate this and is getting even
- If I don't correct her/him now, this will go on forever

Again, the purpose of getting to know these thoughts is to become successful at coaching yourself more effectively through conflicts so that you can better reduce the impact of anger and irritability on your relationships and personal goals.

You Don't Have to Solve This Issue Right Now

Anger can amplify the perceived importance of an issue to the neglect of other important life considerations. It feels important, it has the full pressure of irritable mood behind it, but it is crucial to remember—you don't need to solve the issue now. No matter how important the issue feels it is always important to give yourself time to cool down and consider other strategies to solve the issue at hand.

> *It is always important to give yourself time to cool down and consider other strategies to solve the issue at hand.*

For example, to get out of a conflict quickly and buy time to think things through, you might say:

> *This really upsets me. Let me think about this problem, and then we can talk about it more at a later time. I want to work out a better way of dealing with this.*

The goal is keep others (e.g., your friends, family, coworkers) engaged in wanting to work things out with you. Buy yourself time to see how much extra irritation might be due to a mood episode rather than a result of the conflict at hand. You can always come back to this problem later. There is no reason to act like the present is the crucial moment for solving this issue. Remember, you always have time to devote to anger in the future if you choose, but *you only have right now to prevent a current angry outburst.*

Also, once it becomes clear to you that you are in a period of irritability, you will want to think about what events or meetings you might like to cancel. Some individuals choose to take a sick day at times of increased irritability. By staying home, or rescheduling the most crucial family events or work meetings, you can reduce the likelihood that these events will go badly. In short, invest in your future by making sure that brief periods of irritability do not have a long-term effect by reducing the opportunities for damaging arguments.

Beware of Win/Lose Thinking

Thinking about having to win an argument can prevent you from making more useful choices in a time of irritability and anger. Irritability itself fuels a sense of needing a *win now.* Even when you know intellectually that stopping an argument might be the best option, your irritability may keep you in the mood to prolong the conflict. Don't do it! When feeling irritable, we would like you to remember the following:

> *You don't have to win this argument; instead you need to maximize how well your life is going.*

Sometimes, the best way to truly *finish* an argument well is to save yourself the *guilt and regret* that comes from an overblown conflict. When you cool down, you may realize that there were other alternatives for handling the conflict that would not have led to so many hurt feelings, disrupted friendships, or professional challenges. In helping yourself get out of an argument gracefully, keep in mind the following thoughts that may keep you locked into an argument in a way that does not serve you well.

- I can't let her/him win
- I can't let them get away with this
- I can't lose
- I know I have a point somewhere in here; I am going to force him/her to get it

Remember to Value your Life Goals, Even When Angry

Anger and irritability increase the sense of *I need*. We want you to be able to key into this feeling when you are irritable and angry, but then to use this feeling to guide you toward effective and calm action. For example, when angry, you might think the following:

> *I am frustrated. I can feel my irritability humming along, and I can feel the urge to pick a fight. But I know how it feels after the argument, or a few days later when my mood is different. Even though I have the urge to pick a fight, what would serve me better than having extra conflict?*

The crucial question we want you to ask yourself is the last one, "What can I do now that would *serve me* better than having a conflict?"

In trying to find an answer to this question, don't forget to enlist the help of those who care about you. You don't always have to deal with anger or irritability on your own; find a way to defuse an argumentative evening before it starts. Two examples are provided here that illustrate ways in which you may want to notify a loved one that you are more on edge, and to ask for help in having a better evening either with your loved one (example 1) or on your own (example 2).

I am really having a bad day with lots of frustration and irritability I would love to sit down and talk about ways we can make the evening go well. I may not be in a very good mood, but I bet we can work together to make the evening go better than it might otherwise go.

I am really having a bad day with lots of frustration and irritability. This might be a good evening for me to find a way to entertain myself alone, because I don't want my irritability to affect the family or you. How can we plan the evening so that we both get some nice break time?

In summary, irritability and anger occur frequently with the mood episodes of bipolar disorder. We want you to be ready for these emotions and the thoughts that go along with them. By being ready for the thoughts that intensify anger and keep you engaged in arguments, we hope you will become better at defusing these patterns. Particularly when you are feeling irritable, we want you to treat yourself well. Chapter 7, focusing on planning pleasant events, may serve you well at these times.

Focusing on Life Goals

By its nature, bipolar disorder disrupts life goals and daily plans. Although episodes of mania are responsible for dramatic disruptions—the hospitalization that interfered with the completion of a semester of school, the financial crisis that dominated the marital agenda, or the angry outbursts that led to a job dismissal—depressed moods lead to more longstanding interference with the motivations, goals, relationships, and work habits of individuals with bipolar disorder and their families. Depending on the length and severity of these mood episodes, job functioning may be interrupted, relationships may be strained, friendships may lapse, and educational or social plans may be put off. Accordingly, during periods of stability, individuals with bipolar disorder may have a sense of needing to *catch up* with life agendas that have been disrupted.

We Want to Caution against This Strategy

If we would try to identify one overarching principle to keep in mind relative to the life disruptions of bipolar disorder it is, you don't *get behind* in life; you *experience* life. Life events can always take a linear, planned life and make it more unexpected, more curvilinear, more like the zigzagged course toward goals depicted in Figure 11.1. Mood episodes are such events, and as those with the disorder know well, bipolar brings about multiple mood episodes.

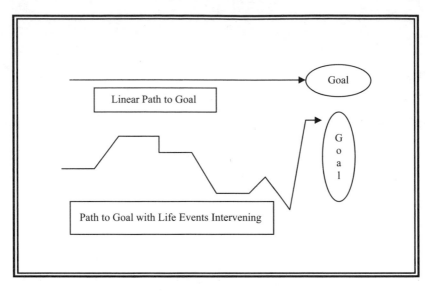

Figure 11.1 *Paths to Life Goals*

Rather than being useful, the strategy of trying to make up for lost time increases stress, guilt, and anxiety, and exaggerates the importance of every interaction and event. In other words, trying too hard to *catch up* in life is a way to increase some of the very mood problems that led to life disruptions in the first place.

But What Is the Alternative?

We recommend two primary strategies. First, we want you to be vigilant to the overly critical and self-defeating thinking patterns that were reviewed in Chapter 8. Be mindful of these patterns especially relative to how you talk to yourself about your life goals. In particular we want you to avoid "I should have..." statements like, "I should have a better [house, car, lover, job, retirement fund, etc.]." These *should* statements tend to direct attention away from some of the larger goals people talk about—wanting to achieve something in life, wanting a human connection, and wanting to have some fun along the way—and over-focus attention on specific markers that are only indirectly linked to these larger goals. Using these arbitrary markers of *should* leads to a sense of being behind, and worse, a sense of having to catch up.

As a second strategy, we want you to acknowledge that bipolar disorder may change the pacing by which you go after life goals. In short, we encourage you to plan your life goals in relation to strategies that most reduce the likelihood of a new episode. All of the previous chapters include attention to this goal. For example, helping you think about medications as tools, problem-solving skills, and communication skills are all designed to help minimize the impact of bipolar disorder on your life. In the same way, we want you to think about honing your attention to the step-by-step movement toward the goals that you think are most important.

The worksheets provided allow you to consider the goals you think are particularly important for the coming year. In thinking through these goals, consider the social, relationship, financial, educational, work, and family domains.

The starting point for considering these goals is important. Please do not start with the goals you want *if your life unfolds ideally.* Instead, attend to *where you are now,* and attend to the several life goals that would make you feel that you are progressing in the direction that you want. In particular, we want you to use the phrase, "Given where I am now, I would like to devote effort to _____ _____." The worksheets that follow are designed to help you with this process.

Self-Guided Care: Achieving Goals Using Pacing

The purpose of this form is to help you think through your long-term goals and to formulate a step-by-step plan for achieving them. In addition to helping you identify and arrange the intermediate steps necessary for achieving larger goals, this worksheet is designed to remind you that achieving your goals is a process that unfolds slowly over time.

Please identify, for this year, a few goals that seem important to you. Please list these goals and then consider and write down why the goals seem important. You may also want to discuss some of these goals with family or friends.

Goal 1: _____

Why does this matter to you (watch out for *should* statements):

_____

_____

_____

Goal 2: _____

Why does this matter to you (watch out for *should* statements):

_____

_____

_____

Goal 3: _____

Why does this matter to you (watch out for *should* statements):

_____

_____

_____

Now that you have identified your goals, please use the next worksheet to plan the intermediate steps that are important for ensuring that you are on track for achieving your larger goals. Please use a separate sheet for each of your larger goals.

Steps to Goal Attainment

Long-term goal:

_____

_____

_____

Short-term goal:

Short-term goal:

Short-term goal:

Short-term goal:

NOW Your current situation:

_____

_____

_____

12

Mood Charting

Why Is Mood Charting Important?

Mood charting is recommended because it enables you to detect early signs of changes in your mood and communicate this information to your care providers. Mood charting can also help you and your treatment team to intervene early to prevent severe episodes.

> *Mood charting can help you detect early signs of changes in your mood.*

An advantage of mood charting is that you become more familiar with the patterning of your mood and your personal triggers for mood changes. For this reason, there is a place on your mood chart to note your daily stressors. There is also space to track your medication doses. Also, disruptions in sleep have the potential for triggering episodes; the mood chart also will help you to watch out for early changes or disruptions in your sleep cycle and to intervene early in collaboration with your clinician.

The mood chart not only has immediate value in summarizing your mood and stressors for your clinician, but it also has value as a record over time. The longer you keep a consistent mood record, the more you can potentially discover about the natural patterns and triggers

Name________________________________

Mood Chart
Month/Year

TREATMENTS
(Enter number of tablets taken each day only)

___ mg	___ mg	Antipsychotic ___ mg	Antidepressant ___ mg	Anticonvulsant ___ mg	Benzodiazepine ___ mg	Lithium ___ mg	Psychotherapy	Daily Notes
								Weight

Figure 12.1 ***Mood Chart***

MOOD
Rate with 2 marks each day to indicate best and worst

Depressed   **WNL**   **Elevated**

0 = none
1 = mild
2 = moderate
3 = severe

Irritability	Anxiety	Hours Slept Last Night	Severe — Significant Impairment NOT ABLE TO WORK	Mod. — Significant Impairment ABLE TO WORK	Mild — Without significant Impairment	MOOD NOT DEFINITELY ELEVATED OR DEPRESSED / NO SYMPTOMS / Circle date to indicate Menses	Mild — Without significant Impairment	Mod. — Significant Impairment ABLE TO WORK	Severe — Significant Impairment NOT ABLE TO WORK	Psychotic Symptoms Strange Ideas, Hallucinations
						1				
						2				
						3				
						4				
						5				
						6				
						7				
						8				
						9				
						10				
						11				
						12				
						13				
						14				
						15				
						16				
						17				
						18				
						19				
						20				
						21				
						22				
						23				
						24				
						25				
						26				
						27				
						28				
						29				
						30				
						31				

for your mood episodes. As such, think of the completion of the daily mood chart as an investment in your future. By making mood chart-ing a regular part of your routine, you and your clinician will have a wealth of information in the future for un-derstanding your pattern of mood changes, and this pattern may aid in your future treatment planning.

> *The mood chart can take as little as 20–30 seconds a day to complete.*

Completing Your Mood Chart

At first glance, the mood chart can appear complicated. This is a very common reaction. However, the mood chart can take as little as 20–30 seconds a day to complete. The directions that follow will help you to fill out your mood chart.

At the start of the day

- Simply record the number of hours of sleep you got last night.

At the end of the day

- Rate your mood, making two ratings—the highest and lowest your mood reached during the day. If your mood did not fluctu-ate, these two ratings may be one and the same. The abbreviation WNL stands for *within normal limits* and refers to a stable or normal mood state.
- Rate your anxiety: None = 0; Mild = 1; Moderate = 2; Severe = 3.
- Rate your irritability: None = 0; Mild = 1; Moderate = 2; Severe = 3.
- Make notes about any stressful or positive events that occurred during the day.
- Record the number of tablets of each medication actually taken.

On a monthly basis

- Record your weight.
- For women, circle the dates when menstruating.

Bring the Mood Chart to Every Clinical Visit

As part of creating a collaborative working relationship with your clinician, we recommend establishing a policy of making the review of the mood chart a part of every session. By showing your clinician your mood chart at the start of each session, you will have more time to focus on issues of importance to you. Most importantly, the mood chart will enable you and your treatment team to maximize the likelihood of good treatment outcomes by keeping close track of symptom patterns over time. The mood chart gives you another tool for maintaining awareness and control over the course of your disorder.

13

Creating a Treatment Contract

Why Contract?

As part of your management of your bipolar disorder, we recommend the use of a written care plan or treatment contract. The treatment contract gives you an opportunity to decide what you want to happen when you are ill. Designing this plan when you are well allows you to specify which management strategies are preferable to cope with severe episodes. This process involves selecting and educating a support system that will participate with you on your treatment contract. Recall from Chapter 1 that your support system may include your doctors, your family members, spouse or significant other, friends, coworkers, and so on. It is important that your support system receive information about bipolar disorder. They can read this book and, most importantly, listen to you about your specific symptoms. You may also invite your support system to attend one of your meetings with your psychiatrist or therapist.

> *The treatment contract gives you an opportunity to decide what you want to happen when you are ill.*

To involve your support system, you must specify ways in which they can be helpful to you during acute episodes. You also may wish to give permission to your support system to contact your treatment team when they detect early symptoms of mania.

We would like you to empower your support system by instructing them to anticipate problems and informing them of the types of reactions and responses you would want them to make. By planning ahead when you are feeling relatively well, you maintain maximal control. Your support team will become agents of *your plan,* not people imposing restrictions on you.

By writing a treatment contract, you and your family members will have an action plan to use in case of future episodes. The treatment contract will enable you to take part in the planning and to exercise choice and control regarding what will happen throughout the course of your bipolar mood disorder and its treatment. Once the treatment contract is signed, your clinicians and family members or support system become agents of your plan, not people controlling your decisions. This approach will allow you to plan ahead during periods of calm in anticipation of the periods of stormy weather that may lie ahead.

Format of the Contract

Your individualized treatment contract begins with a review of the purpose of the contract and an identification of your support team. Then, you specify the characteristic thoughts, feelings, behaviors, and early warning signs for your episodes of depression. Keeping in mind that the symptoms of depression can vary from person to person, you want to personalize the treatment contract to reflect your experience of depression. Next, you specify a plan for coping with depression by stating ways in which your support system can be helpful to you.

Finally, you note the thoughts, feelings, and behaviors and early warning signs of hypomania and mania. You specify a plan for coping with mania or hypomania, giving specific instructions to the members of your support system. For example, instructions might include, "Call my doctor," or "Take away my credit cards." You may also want to specify who initiates the plan for mania. It is often your family or support system who will first recognize the signs of mania. You can also include other modules that target high-risk behaviors, such as substance abuse, bulimia, gambling, and so on, if these are problematic for you.

Your Contract

The contract on the following pages is both a guide for you to use in developing your personalized treatment contract and a kind of generic contract that you may want to fill out so you can have a plan in place while you work on a more personalized plan. Use it to reach the goal of getting your first treatment contract written. As you learn more about your condition and what works or doesn't work for you, the contract can be revised.

Use the following template as a guide. As you personalize the contract to reflect your individuality, feel free to cross out any text you feel is inappropriate or add items you think will be helpful. Your contract should reflect your preferences and should incorporate as much about what you know about yourself as possible.

The most important thing about having a plan is making sure you and everyone who agrees to participate in it actually follow the plan. As you gain experience with this approach to treatment, you will see that knowing who and what you can count on can be the glue that keeps everything together.

Treatment Contract

The purpose of this contract is to organize my care for bipolar disorder, with attention to both the prevention of mood episodes and the efficient treatment of these episodes should they occur. My first step in guiding my care is the selection of my support team. The team members should include people with whom I have regular contact, who can help me identify episodes should they occur and help me put into practice some of the tools discussed in previous chapters of this book.

(Select members of your treatment team to be part of your support team; for example, you may select your psychiatrist, psychologist, social worker, or primary care physician. Other team members may be drawn from the support network identified by you in Chapter 1.)

Treatment Contract: Support Team

Role/relationship	Name	Contact information
My psychiatrist	_____	Phone: _____
My therapist	_____	Phone: _____
My PCP	_____	Phone: _____
_____	_____	Phone: _____
_____	_____	Phone: _____
_____	_____	Phone: _____

My second step in developing this contract is to identify tools I will use to help control my bipolar disorder so that I can best pursue my life goals. Many of these tools have been identified in previous chapters. My goal now is to identify some of the tools that I want to plan to use.

For every tool or strategy listed, please place a checkmark next to the ones you plan to incorporate as a part of your treatment contract.

Monitor My Mood for Early Intervention

Signs of depression and mania are listed in Chapter 2. In addition to these symptoms, I know from my own patterns that I should watch out for the following signs.

Depressed thoughts_____
_____
_____

Depressed symptoms_____
_____
_____

Depressed behavior_____
_____
_____

Hypomanic thoughts_____
_____
_____

Hypomanic symptoms_____
_____
_____

Hypomanic behaviors_____
_____
_____

Take Early Action if I Notice Signs of Depression or Mania

Contact my psychiatrist at phone no. _____.
Contact my therapist at phone no. _____.
Contact my support person at phone no. _____.
Maintain a regular schedule of sleep and activities.
Maintain a regular schedule of pleasant events.

Evaluate my thoughts for negative or hyperpositive thinking.

Talk with my family about ways to cope.

Limit my alcohol use and avoid all nonmedication drugs.

Other _____.

Other _____.

Other _____.

Other _____.

To Take Active Steps to Keep My Mood in the Desired Range

Take all medications as prescribed by my doctor.

Maintain regular appointments with my psychiatrist at ——— / month.

Maintain regular appointments with my therapist at ——— / month.

Keep a regular sleep schedule.

Maintain a schedule including at least three valued activities each day as a buffer against stress.

Avoid excessive use of alcohol.

Avoid all use of illicit drugs.

Use no alcohol for the next 30 days.

Use no recreational drugs for the next 30 days.

Keep a perspective on my thoughts and evaluate my thoughts for accuracy.

Share with my family information on communication styles that may reduced stress.

Other _____.

Other _____.

Other _____.

Other _____.

Contact the Following People Should I Ever Have Strong Suicidal Thoughts

Contact my psychiatrist at phone no. _____.

Contact my therapist at phone no. _____.

Contact my support person at phone no. _____.

Other action _____.

Keep Myself Safe Until I Can Be Seen or Go to a Local Emergency Room If I Ever Fear I May Act on Suicidal Thoughts.

If I Start to Become Depressed, I Would Like My Support Team to:

Talk to me about my symptoms (who _____)

Make plans for a pleasant event (who _____)

Discuss ways to reduce stress (who _____)

Make sure I am taking my medication (who _____)

Call my doctor if I am unable to (who _____)

Other _____

Other _____

Other _____

If I Start to Become Manic, I Would Like My Support Team to:

Talk to me about my symptoms (who _____)

Talk to me about reducing activities (who _____)

Allow me to be alone if I am irritable (who _____)

Take care of the kids/pets/other (who _____)

Take away my credit cards (who _____)

Take away my car keys (who _____)

Take me to the hospital (preferred hospital _____)

Other _____

Other _____

Other _____

I understand that this contract is designed by me so that I can take an active role in my treatment. My goal is to maximize my control by arranging for my support team to take care of me. So that any future decisions are well considered, I agree to change this contract only after giving two weeks written notice to all parties to this contract.

Signatures for Contracting Individuals

_____	_____
Signature Date	Signature Date
_____	_____
Signature Date	Signature Date

14

Improving Wellbeing

Our goals for this book were to provide you with a wide range of strategies for better managing bipolar disorder. Most of the strategies in this book were directed at reducing symptoms of mood disorders or reducing the stresses that can make mood episodes more likely. It would be a mistake, however, to focus on only the reduction of symptoms. It is also important to focus on the enhancement of positive emotions. In particular, we would like you to attend to those moments when you feel satisfied and pleasantly happy. We refer to these moments as periods of wellbeing.

With the term wellbeing we are referring to moments when you feel satisfied and happy. We are not referring to moments of particular excitement, achievement, or superiority, but of much quieter moments of wellbeing. This distinction is important, especially with respect to periods of hypomania. By focusing on wellbeing instead of hypomania, we are asking you to note and track periods of pleasantness (versus elation), satisfaction (versus excitement) and happiness (versus bliss). Most formally, we would like you to start a wellbeing diary, where, no matter what

> *Start a well-being diary so you can refer back to moments of pleasantness, satisfaction, and happiness in your life.*

your dominant mood was, you are to select and write about the period of greatest wellbeing during each day.

Buy a journal or notebook that appeals to you and represents who you are and use it as your wellbeing diary. Keep your diary in a handy place for nightly entries. The goal is to describe the feeling of wellbeing and the events (situations, interactions, or thoughts) that led to it. It is important to do this with some regularity so that over time, you develop a log that can guide you to the pleasant moments in your life.

In addition to recording this information, we want to make sure that you become adept at *echoing* and increasing these moments. Echoing refers to the process of making sure that a pleasant event has reverberations during the day; that during periods where you might otherwise be daydreaming about problems, you take a moment to reflect on a period of wellbeing (from earlier that day or a previous day). In that way, the wellbeing period will echo across the day allowing you to relive these feelings. This echoing will naturally enhance your interest in planning additional activities of this sort. In fact, we encourage you to ask yourself the following questions when thinking back on a particular period of wellbeing.

- How did the period of wellbeing come about?
- What brought it to an end?
- What seems like a good idea for having (planning for) another moment like this?
- What seems like a good idea for making that moment of wellbeing last longer or be better echoed during the day?

The good news is that by attending to your periods of wellbeing, tracking them, and putting effort into expanding them, you will be likely to reduce the recurrence of depressed mood, as well as treat more subtle symptoms of depression that did not go away as the more severe mood episode lifted. And we especially like that these benefits come not from trying to reduce negative aspects of your life, but instead from attending to the positive aspects of your life. In this way, wellbeing interventions are much more like the watering the flowers not the weeds approach from Chapter 9. Placing attention on what is working rather than what is not working is a nice way of creating change.

Start your wellbeing diary as soon as possible, regardless of whether you are in a positive or negative mood. Even when you are depressed, it is both possible and beneficial to track the moments in a day when you do have relative wellbeing. When down and when feeling better, we want you to be good at noticing the range of situations and events that may increase wellbeing (e.g., when alone, when with others, during an activity, spontaneously when you did not expect it, etc.) and use this information to enhance these feelings in your life.

Index

friends, 4
 suicidal thoughts and, 73
 thought accuracy and, 70
frustration, 89

genetics, 13
Geodon, 22
goals. *See also* life goals
 irritability and anger and, 84–86
 long-term, 94
 pacing of, 94
 remembering, 88–89
 setting, 4
 short-term, 95
 starting point of, 93
 steps to attainment of, 95
 taking medications and, 28
 of treatment contract, 109–10
guilt, 87–88

Haldol, 22
hallucinations, 21
happiness, 111
hobbies, 55–56
 for mood stabilizing, 58–61
homework, 43
hospitals, 47
 suicidal thoughts and, 72
hyperpositive thinking, 69–70
hypomania
 anxiolytics and, 23
 Bipolar II and, 10–11
 Bipolar NOS and, 11
 cyclothymia and, 11
 definition of, 8
 depression *v.,* 69
 DSM-IV-TR and, 6
 irritability and anger and, 84
 symptom summary, 7*t*
 warning signs, 105
 wellbeing *v.,* 111

idealism, 93
IEP. *See* Individualized Education
 Plan

illness, periods of, 3
individuality, 105
Individualized Education Plan
 (IEP), 43
insomnia, 18, 23. *See also* sleep
instant messenger (IM), 46
instructions, for support
 teams, 105
internet, 46
interpersonal psychotherapy
 (IPT), 35
interventions
 early, 107
 wellbeing, 113
IPT. *See* interpersonal
 psychotherapy
irritability, 83–85
 mood charting and, 99*f*
 problem solving and, 86–87
 rating, 100
 remembering goals and, 88–89
 thinking patterns and, 85–86
 win/lose thinking and, 87–88
Isoptin, 19

journals, 111–12

ketamine, 66
Klonopin, 23

Lamictal, 19
lamotrigine, 19
learning disabilities, 39
 college planning and, 44
 instruction for, 43
leisure, 54–56
life disruptions, 91
life goals, 91–92
 pacing of, 93
 paths to, 92*f*
 strategies, 92–93
listening, effective, 78–79
lithium, 19
 mood charting and, 98*f*
Lithobid, 19